6:30 WED - TRIPP

1 SAMUEL

REFORMED EXPOSITORY BIBLE STUDIES

A Companion Series to the Reformed Expository Commentaries

Series Editors

Daniel M. Doriani
Iain M. Duguid
Richard D. Phillips
Philip Graham Ryken

1 Samuel: A King after God's Own Heart
Esther & Ruth: The Lord Delivers and Redeems
Daniel: Faith Enduring through Adversity
Matthew: Making Disciples for the Nations (two volumes)
Luke: Knowing for Sure (two volumes)
Galatians: The Gospel of Free Grace
Ephesians: The Glory of Christ in the Life of the Church
Hebrews: Standing Firm in Christ
James: Portrait of a Living Faith

Coming in 2022

Song of Songs: Friendship on Fire
John: The Word Incarnate (two volumes)
Philippians: To Live Is Christ

1 SAMUEL

A KING AFTER GOD'S OWN HEART

A 13-LESSON STUDY

REFORMED EXPOSITORY
BIBLE STUDY

JON NIELSON
and **RICHARD D. PHILLIPS**

P U B L I S H I N G
P.O. BOX 817 • PHILLIPSBURG • NEW JERSEY 08865-0817

Unless otherwise indicated, Scripture quotations are from the ESV® Bible (The Holy Bible, English Standard Version®), copyright © 2001 by Crossway, a publishing ministry of Good News Publishers. Used by permission. All rights reserved.

Scripture quotations marked (NIV) are taken from the Holy Bible, New International Version®, NIV®. Copyright © 1973, 1978, 1984, 2011 by Biblica, Inc.™ Used by permission of Zondervan. All rights reserved worldwide. www.zondervan.com The "NIV" and "New International Version" are trademarks registered in the United States Patent and Trademark Office by Biblica, Inc.™

All boxed quotations are taken from Richard D. Phillips's *1 Samuel* in the Reformed Expository Commentary series. Page numbers in quotations refer to that source.

The quoted material at the end of the boxed quotation on page 96 is from Dale Ralph Davis, *1 Samuel: Looking on the Heart* (Fearn, Ross-shire, UK: Christian Focus, 2000), 174.

ISBN: 978-1-62995-838-5 (pbk)
ISBN: 978-1-62995-839-2 (ePub)

Printed in the United States of America

CONTENTS

SERIES INTRODUCTION

Studying the Bible will change your life. This is the consistent witness of Scripture and the experience of people all over the world, in every period of church history.

King David said, "The law of the LORD is perfect, reviving the soul; the testimony of the LORD is sure, making wise the simple; the precepts of the LORD are right, rejoicing the heart; the commandment of the LORD is pure, enlightening the eyes" (Ps. 19:7–8). So anyone who wants to be wiser and happier, and who wants to feel more alive, with a clearer perception of spiritual reality, should study the Scriptures.

Whether we study the Bible alone or with other Christians, it will change us from the inside out. The Reformed Expository Bible Studies provide tools for biblical transformation. Written as a companion to the Reformed Expository Commentary, this series of short books for personal or group study is designed to help people study the Bible for themselves, understand its message, and then apply its truths to daily life.

Each Bible study is introduced by a pastor-scholar who has written a full-length expository commentary on the same book of the Bible. The individual chapters start with the summary of a Bible passage, explaining **The Big Picture** of this portion of God's Word. Then the questions in **Getting Started** introduce one or two of the passage's main themes in ways that connect to life experience. These questions may be especially helpful for group leaders in generating lively conversation.

Understanding the Bible's message starts with seeing what is actually there, which is where **Observing the Text** comes in. Then the Bible study provides a longer and more in-depth set of questions entitled **Understanding the Text**. These questions carefully guide students through the entire passage, verse by verse or section by section.

It is important not to read a Bible passage in isolation, but to see it in the wider context of Scripture. So each Bible study includes two **Bible Connections** questions that invite readers to investigate passages from other places in Scripture—passages that add important background, offer valuable contrasts or comparisons, and especially connect the main passage to the person and work of Jesus Christ.

The next section is one of the most distinctive features of the Reformed Expository Bible Studies. The authors believe that the Bible teaches important doctrines of the Christian faith, and that reading biblical literature is enhanced when we know something about its underlying theology. The questions in **Theology Connections** identify some of these doctrines by bringing the Bible passage into conversation with creeds and confessions from the Reformed tradition, as well as with learned theologians of the church.

Our aim in all of this is to help ordinary Christians apply biblical truth to daily life. **Applying the Text** uses open-ended questions to get people thinking about sins that need to be confessed, attitudes that need to change, and areas of new obedience that need to come alive by the power and influence of the Holy Spirit. Finally, each study ends with a **Prayer Prompt** that invites Bible students to respond to what they are learning with petitions for God's help and words of praise and gratitude.

You will notice boxed quotations throughout the Bible study. These quotations come from one of the volumes in the Reformed Expository Commentary. Although the Bible study can stand alone and includes everything you need for a life-changing encounter with a book of the Bible, it is also intended to serve as a companion to a full commentary on the same biblical book. Reading the full commentary is especially useful for teachers who want to help their students answer the questions in the Bible study at a deeper level, as well as for students who wish to further enrich their own biblical understanding.

The people who worked together to produce this series of Bible studies have prayed that they will engage you more intimately with Scripture, producing the kind of spiritual transformation that only the Bible can bring.

Philip Graham Ryken
Coeditor of the Reformed Expository Commentary series

INTRODUCING 1 SAMUEL

First Samuel introduces one of the most romantic and heroic figures in all of Scripture: David, the man of faith. Yet the book is about so much more than the life of David. It would be better to say that the **main purpose** of the books of Samuel is to provide a key guide to one of God's great redemptive acts in history: establishing his covenant with David to erect the eternal throne on which his Son and David's heir, Jesus Christ, now sits. After the dramatic events of Israel's exodus and the conquest of the land of Canaan under Joshua, God's next step was to establish the Davidic kingship as a type of the true kingdom that would come through Christ. The book of Judges, which bridges the gap between Joshua and Samuel, informs us that it was because "there was no king in Israel" that "everyone did what was right in his own eyes" (Judg. 21:25). A true leader was needed who would elevate God's people out of the mire of their sin. Next, the book of Ruth directs our thoughts to Bethlehem, from which redemption will come, and concludes with the birth of David's near ancestor—Obed, the father of Jesse (see Ruth 4:17). The questions that Judges and Ruth raise—Where is the true king? What will come out of this gracious union between Ruth and Boaz?—are answered in the narrative of 1 Samuel.

Because 1 Samuel covers a crucial time of historical transition, David is hardly the only fascinating and important person we meet in this book. Indeed, 1 Samuel's eponymous prophet and judge is one of the most important figures in all of Scripture. Samuel's importance is signaled by the circumstances of his birth and by the experiences of the spiritually bountiful Hannah, a woman whose feminine piety foreshadows that of Jesus's young mother, Mary. Samuel personally bridges the era of the judges and the coming era of kings, as he anoints young David and oversees the abortive kingship that God introduces through Saul—himself one of the more provocative figures in Scripture. Commended for kingship by his good looks and great height, Saul is David's shadow. He is the epitome of the man-centered, self-reliant kingship that worldly people often admire but that God rejects. Samuel contrasts David with Saul when he speaks these notable words: "Man looks on the outward appearance, but the LORD looks on the heart" (1 Sam. 16:7).

David bursts onto the narrative of 1 Samuel in chapter 17, when as a young man he appears at the scene of battle and is aghast at the humiliation visited upon God's people by the Philistine giant Goliath. By slaying the giant with a single shot from his sling, David not only changes his own life forever but also highlights the theme of faith that is so important to this book. And yet David's faith is not the source of Israel's deliverance. Rather it is God's anointing—which makes David a preview of the Messiah who was yet to come—that provides salvation. Although David is a model of faith for Christians today, his faith doesn't so much provide an example of what we can do if we only believe but rather displays the salvation that God provides through Jesus Christ to people who trust in him and his Word.

One of the more enjoyable **features** of 1 Samuel is the covenant friendship between David and Saul's son, Jonathan. Together over the course of many years and through many trials, these men of like spirit encouraged one another as they placed their confidence in the promises of God. Jonathan is an extraordinary figure—one of whom the sacred narrative records no vices. How different life in the church would be if more believers imbibed the selfless, loving spirit of this great man. Although Jonathan held a high station and had been quite the hero prior to meeting David, he subordinated himself to God's purpose regarding the true anointed king. 1 Samuel 18 tells how Jonathan loved David for his faith and did everything he could to promote him—even divesting himself of honor and privilege. Over the years, Jonathan struggled to balance his faithfulness to his increasingly mad father, King Saul, with his faith in what God said and the loyalty to young David that this demanded. That Jonathan managed to maintain this balance—though it cost him his own life—reinforces his inspiring example. When the apostle Paul wrote many years later that the only thing that ultimately matters is "faith expressing itself through love" (Gal. 5:6 NIV), he might easily have used Jonathan's life as an illustration.

It remains the case, however, that David himself dominates the narrative of 1 Samuel. He presents a type of Jesus Christ—the greater Anointed One through whom God's promises to David would finally come true. Like Jesus, David exercises his faith throughout many scenes of painful trial and sorrow. This is not to say that he consistently excels in showing faith; indeed, throughout the years of persecution he experiences at Saul's hands, we can track the ups and downs of a life that wavers between faith and forgetfulness. The same man who stands before the giant in the pristine faith of youth later resorts to feigning insanity after he foolishly seeks refuge in Goliath's Philistine hometown. Finally despairing of ever escaping Saul, David departs from Israel altogether and finds refuge as a bandit leader under a Philistine lord. He is delivered from ruin only by the providence of God—albeit through a tragedy that reduces him to tears. In short, David is a completely human figure who struggles to act consistently in faith while facing the most daunting trials—all of which serve to refine his character for the kingship that will come to him in 2 Samuel. It is at his best, when he acts in the strength of the Lord and through the means of faith, that David meets his generation's need for spiritual leadership—and is a type of the Savior Jesus Christ.

The material of 1 Samuel may be organized into three main **sections**. The first section, consisting of chapters 1 through 7, presents the saving power of God in contrast to the spiritual impotence of his people. Its chief figure is Samuel. His mother's barrenness reflects the spiritual condition of the people as a whole; and yet when Hannah prays in faith, God brings forth life from her barren womb and provides a leader for the nation. During this time, the priesthood has become especially debased due to the poor leadership of the high priest Eli and the wantonness of his sons, Hophni and Phinehas. Thinking that God's power can be stored in a box, these false priests lead the Israelite army out into battle—only for the Lord to deliver the ark of the covenant into the hands of the victorious Philistines. No sooner has this catastrophe fallen on Israel than God's power appears in the midst of the Philistines—humbling their false god Dagon and visiting such wrath on the ungodly people that they hastily return the ark to Israel. This opening section concludes with the restoration of Israel at Mizpah, which showcases the grace that God gives for repentance, which in turn leads Samuel to raise the Ebenezer stone in remembrance of God's faithfulness.

The second main section of 1 Samuel, which consists of chapters 8 to 15, tells of King Saul. We watch in bewilderment as the people respond to Samuel's approaching death not by renewing their faith in what God says but by demanding to have "a king to judge us like all the nations" (1 Sam. 8:5). A broken-hearted Samuel appeals to God, but the Lord tells him to give the people what they want. Therefore, an impressive person who is strong in the flesh is, to the acclamation of the tribes, brought forth to be king. Saul has virtues to go along with his height and strong looks, and they produce some signal victories early in his reign. It soon becomes clear, however, that he is incapable of trusting God's commands. When Saul willfully violates God's commands, Samuel announces that his kingdom will be torn away and speaks the notable words "to obey is better than sacrifice" (1 Sam. 15:22).

The final section of 1 Samuel, which covers chapters 16 to 31, introduces the man after God's own heart (see 1 Sam. 13:14): the young hero David. As we first encounter him in his youth as a devoted but overlooked shepherd boy, we see that God has been preparing David through early lessons in faith. Anointed as the chosen king by Samuel and filled with the onrushing Holy Spirit, he burns with a passion for the glory of God. The sight of young David standing courageously before the massive Goliath, "in the name of the LORD of hosts, the God of the armies of Israel, whom you have defied" (1 Sam. 17:45), is a scene that readers can hardly forget. Armed with faith, empowered by God's Spirit, and playing a role that would ultimately be filled by Jesus Christ, David strikes down the foe and delivers the people of God. He immediately becomes a national figure—a development for which he is less than prepared. Armed with God's power, he leads Israel's soldiers to great victories but fails to perceive the annoyance and then hatred that his preeminence is stirring in Saul's jealous heart. Before long, David's early faith is tested and matured when he becomes a fugitive from the irrational, malicious king. The best biblical commentary on the faith he maintained throughout his life of struggle comes from David himself, in poems such as Psalm 27: "The LORD is my light and my salvation; whom shall I fear? The LORD is the stronghold of my life; of whom shall I be afraid?" (Ps. 27:1). The varied experiences throughout which he proves these words true ultimately set before us the kinds of circumstances in which David's heir Jesus Christ would gain true victory.

A study of 1 Samuel is therefore far more than a mere "life of David." The Lord is the true hero of Samuel's books, as he provides Samuel to be the prophet and judge that Israel needs, prepares the ground for David's appearance, and empowers the young champion through the outpouring of his Holy Spirit. Bible students will find this book to be an unforgettable account that is filled with rich and memorable stories. If this study is guiding your first journey through 1 Samuel, I envy you for the sheer enjoyment of the discovery that lies ahead. The trials, prayers, faith, and struggles of the men and women in these pages provide a great deal of help for us as we make our way through a world that has not truly changed even after the passage of so many years. But we must not take our eye off the book's true **subject**: God's incarnate Son, who bore a truly holy heart and whose victories, which he won in the power of faith and the Holy Spirit, accomplished an eternal victory for all those who believe. As Jesus reported in Luke 20:42, David's own profession of faith was lifted to a Savior whom he prophesied would come: "The LORD says to my Lord: 'Sit at my right hand, until I make your enemies your footstool'" (Ps. 110:1). After this study, you will never forget the young David of 1 Samuel. His own expressed desire, however, was for God's people to steadfastly look to the Messiah who would someday come, who now has come, and who is the true object of our faith as we follow the story of 1 Samuel.

Richard D. Phillips
Coeditor of the Reformed Expository Commentary series
Coeditor of the Reformed Expository Bible Study series
Author of *1 Samuel* (REC)

LESSON 1

FROM BARRENNESS TO BIRTH

1 Samuel 1:1–2:10

THE BIG PICTURE

As you begin your study of the book of 1 Samuel, it will be important for you to remember the most immediate historical context for the narrative that is beginning to unfold. God's people have been enduring the era of the judges—a messy and dark season that has involved some positive deliverance . . . along with much sin, idolatry, and rebellion. It has become clear that God's people need someone to lead them well in the areas of worship, obedience, and covenant faithfulness to their God. In a way, the predicament that Hannah faces as a barren woman represents the predicament of Israel as a whole: God's people suffer through the barrenness of leaderless chaos, spiritual darkness, and rampant wickedness.

The passage that you will study today, though, points to how God faithfully provides for his people. He will ultimately provide them a king—but before he does that, he will raise up a final, godly judge: Samuel. Just as the barren Hannah gives birth to a son who has been given to her by God, so the barren Israel will receive a king who has been chosen and anointed by God. Today you will meet Hannah, who lives with a kind and loving husband and yet longs for a son (1:1–8). She pleads to God for the gift of a child and vows that she will commit him to the Lord's service for all the days of his life, and God grants her petition (1:9–20). After committing her son Samuel to service in the temple under the leadership of Eli the priest, Hannah responds to God with a great song of praise (1:21–2:10).

Read 1 Samuel 1:1–2:10.

GETTING STARTED

1. Why do we tend to doubt God during times of waiting? What false views of God are you tempted to embrace when he seems not to be answering your prayers—or at least not answering them in the way you would like?

2. In what surprising ways have you seen God's faithfulness and provision throughout your life? Do you tend to remember to thank him for these times? Why, or why not?

Preparing the Way for the King, pg. 6

The birth of Samuel portended a new age. Just as God would later prepare Israel for her Messiah by sending John the Baptist, God prepared the way for a king after God's own heart . . . by sending Samuel, who was at once the last of Israel's judges and the first of the great line of the prophets who served during Israel's kingdom.

OBSERVING THE TEXT

3. What does the author want us to notice about Hannah's situation? How does the text help to make her a truly human character with whom we can identify?

4. Consider the ways in which the character of God is developed throughout this passage. In what way does he act in Hannah's life? What does Hannah say about God in her prayer?

5. What hints might this passage be offering us about what will happen in the rest of the book? What might cause the reader to expect that Samuel will be significant to the nation of Israel?

UNDERSTANDING THE TEXT

6. Why is it significant for us to remember the historical context of this passage (i.e., the time of the judges)? What does knowing that context contribute to our understanding of the situation that God's people were in during these days?

7. What does the author do to emphasize Hannah's poignant pain in 1:1–8? How would you describe the character of her husband, Elkanah?

8. What makes Hannah's prayer to God bold and specific (1:9–11)? What does the initial response that Eli gives Hannah in verses 12–14 tell you about the spiritual state of Israel during this time? What words of truth and assurance does he ultimately speak to comfort her (1:15–18)?

9. In what way does God answer Hannah's prayer (1:19–20)? What does this tell us about his character? How will this answer to her prayer further go on to provide hope, life, and salvation for the people of Israel?

The Key to Hannah's Prayer, pg. 26

We know that Hannah reasoned in a believing manner, because she did not wait until her prayer was answered to regain a joyful attitude. Her example urges us similarly to find our peace in waiting on the Lord, knowing his mercy and grace. The key to Hannah's prayer is that she knew the Lord.

10. What does Hannah reveal about her character and integrity by committing Samuel to the Lord (1:21–28)? What would have made this extremely difficult for Hannah—as it would have for any mother? What truths about God and his purposes might have been guiding her when she did this?

11. What are the main themes of the prayer of praise that Hannah offers to God in 2:1–10? What actions does she attribute to God? What does she say about his character? How do the themes of this prayer show us glimpses of the God of the gospel, who sends his Son to be the great Savior for his people (note especially verse 10 and its mention of the "anointed")?

BIBLE CONNECTIONS

12. Read Judges 21:25. How does this verse clarify the barren situation that characterized the people of Israel during the days of Hannah and Elkanah? What was the result of Israel's not having a king during this time?

13. Read Philippians 4:6–7—one of the many places within Paul's letters that contain instructions for Christians on prayer. How does Paul instruct followers of Jesus to pray? About what should we pray? What is the clear promise that God offers for those who pray in these ways?

THEOLOGY CONNECTIONS

14. Monica, the mother of the great St. Augustine, prayed for years for her son's conversion while he was living for pleasure, sin, and his own selfish desires—before he finally turned to Christ in faith.[1] In what way can both Monica and Hannah serve as models for us of how to persist in prayer? What must we remember about God's character, sovereignty, and perfect timing as we appeal to him in earnest prayer?

15. Answer 98 of the Westminster Shorter Catechism defines prayer in this way: "Prayer is an offering up of our desires unto God for things agreeable to his will, in the name of Christ, with confession of our sins, and thankful acknowledgment of his mercies." How do you see Hannah serving as a faithful model of this approach to prayer? What can you learn from this brief and clear description of Christian prayer?

---

1. See Richard D. Phillips, *1 Samuel*, Reformed Expository Commentary (Phillipsburg, NJ: 2012), 13.

APPLYING THE TEXT

16. What can this passage teach us regarding the times of waiting and watching we experience when we ask God for specific answers to prayer? What must we remember about God's character and purpose, even when he does not immediately answer our prayers?

17. How does the provision that God makes for Hannah—and for Israel— remind us of the sovereign purposes he has for the good of his people? In what way do you hear "echoes" of the gospel within this passage? How does it foreshadow the coming of an even greater child who would be set apart for God's purposes?

A Fitting Foretelling, pg. 49

Hannah's Song is the first direct reference in the Old Testament to God's promised *Messiah*, which in New Testament Greek is rendered as *Christ*. How appropriate that this promise should come from Hannah's lips! Who better to foretell God's gift of his own Son to be the Savior of sinful mankind than the woman who freely gave her firstborn son to serve the Lord . . . ?

18. How could Hannah serve as a good model for your prayer life? In what way can the joy she experienced, even before her prayer was answered, serve as an example of the joyful trust that you should place in God as well? In what way could her prayer of praise from 2:1–10 shape the way we respond to God for the provision, grace, and forgiveness he has shown us?

PRAYER PROMPT

You have studied the beautiful beginning of the narrative of 1 Samuel, in which the faithfulness God shows to the barren Hannah coincides with the faithfulness he shows to the barren Israel. He will give the barren women a child; he will bring his people a great judge . . . and ultimately an anointed king! Today, as you close your study of this lesson, praise God for the eternal faithfulness he has shown you by giving the gift of the great Anointed One—his Son, Jesus Christ. Ask him to help you to remember this ultimate faithfulness, even as you continue to lay before him the desires of your heart, the pains of your life, and your very real needs. Pray for patience and joy as you trust him and wait to receive his answer—in his time and in his way.

Pb 303
6 10 19

LESSON 2

THE FALL AND RISE
OF A PRIESTHOOD

1 Samuel 2:11–4:1

THE BIG PICTURE

As our last lesson concluded, Hannah kept her vow to the Lord and offered her young son, Samuel, to the full-time service of God. Today we will consider the call that young Samuel receives, which we will see sharply contrasted with God's condemnation of Eli's wicked sons (Hophni and Phineas, though they serve as priests of the people, are consumed with sexual sin and greed)—despite the rebuke that they receive from their father (2:11–26). In response to this, God sends a prophet to Eli to inform him of the coming downfall of his house and line of priests: his sons will die on the same day, and God will raise up another, more faithful priest to serve him and lead his people (2:27–36). As we move on to 1 Samuel 3, we begin to see God fulfilling this prophetic word through the life of the young boy Samuel, who is growing up in the house of the Lord with Eli. God calls out to Samuel in the night; when Samuel finally invites him to speak, God tells him of the judgment that is coming to both Eli and his sons, who have desecrated the priesthood and abandoned their fear of God (3:1–21). The passage for today's lesson concludes with the words of the Lord coming to Samuel with power and then going out from him to "all Israel" (4:1). The contrast that this passage portrays is devastating and striking: the sons of Eli live for sin, self, and pleasure, while God raises up for himself a priest and prophet who will live under the authority of the perfect word that he speaks to his people and will lead the people with holiness and truth.

Read 1 Samuel 2:11–4:1.

GETTING STARTED

1. Why is the moral failure and downfall of religious leaders so demoralizing for Christians? What negative or harmful effects have you seen the fall of Christian leaders have on the lives of followers of Jesus whom you know and love?

2. What, in your opinion, are the characteristics of a good leader in general? What other characteristics would you add to that list if you were describing a good *Christian* leader, specifically? Explain your answer.

A Dramatic Contrast, pg. 61
Young Samuel made quite a contrast to the condemned house of Eli. As God was preparing to tear down, God was also preparing to raise up, providing a godly leader for his forlorn people.

OBSERVING THE TEXT

3. What does the narrator of this passage want the reader to notice about Hophni and Phineas? What does he do to make clear the egregious nature of their sin and corruption?

4. What do you see being repeated within this passage? Why do you think this prophetic word comes to Eli both through the unnamed man of God and through young Samuel?

5. How would you describe Samuel's character, based on this first description we have of him as a young boy? What does he seem to value most? What drives him?

UNDERSTANDING THE TEXT

6. What are the particular sins of Hophni and Phineas, and what makes their sin especially heinous in light of the role they have as priests (2:11–17)? In what way does the narrator quickly contrast young Samuel with the sons of Eli (2:18–21)?

7. How does Eli confront his sons—and what is their response when he does so (2:22–25)? Are there any hints in these verses about the strength or weakness that characterized Eli as a father? How does verse 26 contrast Samuel with Eli's sons yet again?

8. What does the unnamed man of God reveal to Eli about the judgment that is coming against his house and his sons (2:27–36)? What does this prophecy show about God's character and justice as well as about the seriousness of human sin and rebellion? What does God reveal about the plan he has for another priest (2:35–36)?

9. How does Samuel initially respond to the call that he hears—and in what way does Eli guide him to respond to this call, which he himself knows is from the Lord (3:1–10)? What makes this an important moment in the life of young Samuel?

The Importance of a Simple Commitment, pg. 63
The message of godly little Samuel and the wicked sons of Eli is that nothing is ever more important than individual godliness, in godly and gracious families, with a simple commitment to God's Word and to prayer.

10. What is the content of the prophetic word that God speaks to Samuel in 3:11–14? In what way does it agree with the prophetic word from 1 Samuel 2? What is Eli's response to it—and how does this response set him apart spiritually from his own sons (3:15–18)?

11. In what way does the conclusion of this passage demonstrate the power of Samuel's role as a priest and prophet for God's people (3:19–4:1)? In what ways do these verses set him up as a "type" (or picture) of Jesus Christ? How will Jesus go on to fulfill these roles for God's people even more perfectly and fully?

BIBLE CONNECTIONS

12. In Isaiah 55:10–11, we read about the power and effectiveness of God's Word. Consider those verses now. Taking into account the truths that those verses affirm about God's Word, what can we anticipate to be true of Samuel's ministry as he rightly proclaims what God says to his people?

13. Read Hebrews 4:14–16, which portrays Jesus Christ as our great, holy, sinless High Priest. What makes these verses so comforting? How does the comfort that we experience from these verses contrast with the fear and anger that the Israelites whom Hophni and Phineas served might have experienced?

THEOLOGY CONNECTIONS

14. The Westminster Confession of Faith begins with affirmations that Scripture is the very Word of God. The Bible, according to section 1.1, came to us as God intended "for the better preserving and propagating of the truth, and for the more sure establishment and comfort of the Church against the corruption of the flesh, and the malice of Satan and of the world, to commit the same wholly unto writing; which maketh the holy Scripture to be most necessary; those former ways of God's revealing his will unto his people being now ceased." How should these truths about God's Word shape the attitude we have toward it? With what mindset should we read and study the Bible—and how can Samuel serve as a model for us as we do this?

15. The doctrines of the wrath of God and the eternal punishment he decrees are biblical, even though they are difficult for Christians today. How do the words of prophecy that are spoken against the sons of Eli in

this passage confirm those doctrines? Why is the concept of God's just punishment of sin important for Christians to maintain and believe?

APPLYING THE TEXT

16. What ought to serve as a warning for us as we read of the sin and rebellion of Hophni and Phineas? What seemed to be the motivation that characterized their lives, relationships, and even religious service? How can we learn from their sin and mistakes?

17. What attitude concerning the words of God does young Samuel demonstrate in this passage? How should the way he responds to what God says shape our own response to Scripture as we read and study it and hear it preached regularly?

A Credible Servant of God, pg. 72

Samuel as a prophet was able to speak truth to the people in a way that was valid and credible. As we grow in the Lord, hearing God's Word from the Bible and faithfully speaking it to others, our speech will also mark us as true servants of the Lord.

18. In what way does Samuel point us to Jesus Christ, our Savior? As we see God raising Samuel up as a prophet and priest for his people, what truths should we remember about Jesus Christ—our great Prophet and Priest?

PRAYER PROMPT

As you have seen in your study today, Eli's priestly sons—the very men who were set aside to serve and lead the people of God in their worship—chose instead to fulfill their sexual appetites and desires by abusing God's people. In stark contrast to them stands Samuel, who listens humbly to what God says and prepares to speak his message clearly to all Israel. Conclude your study today in prayer by thanking God for the greater Samuel, Jesus Christ, who faithfully reconciles you with God through his sacrificial offering. Then ask God for the humility to listen well to his Word as well as for courage so that you may also speak the gospel with clarity to the world around you.

LESSON 3

GOD OF EVERY NATION

1 Samuel 4:1–5:12

THE BIG PICTURE

We should begin our study of 1 Samuel 4–5 with the prophetic words of chapters 2 and 3 ringing in our ears. Both through unnamed man of God and through young Samuel, God has declared imminent judgment on Eli and his wicked sons—a punishment that is well-deserved, sure, and inevitable. Even so, as the people of God march out in battle against the Philistines at the beginning of chapter 4, they confidently assume that God will continue to bless their efforts—despite the blatant sin of their priestly leaders. When the battle turns against them, they bring the ark of the covenant into their camp, thinking that its presence will serve as a kind of good luck charm against their enemies—only for the Philistines to gain a decisive victory and capture the ark in the process (4:1–11). The sad scene of Eli's death follows; he falls from his chair and breaks his neck when he hears the news of his sons' death and of the capture of the ark (4:12–18). Then, even as the son of Phinehas is born, his mother dies as well, after expressing through the naming of her child the moment of despair that has gripped all of Israel (4:19–22). In the land of the Philistines, however, God makes it clear that he has in no way been defeated by the Philistine gods (5:1–12)! As the idol Dagon falls on his face before the ark of the covenant and plagues break out in every Philistine town where the ark is kept, God demonstrates his universal rule over all nations. He has not been defeated, and his plan for his people will continue—even through judgment on their enemies.

Read 1 Samuel 4:1–5:12.

GETTING STARTED

1. What are some ways in which you have seen people seek to use God or to manipulate him for their own purposes? At what points of your life and your walk with him have *you* been guilty of doing this?

2. In what ways has God used challenges, suffering, or pain to discipline you as his child and to strengthen your faith in Jesus? How does he demonstrate his love for his people through discipline?

The Theology of the Cross, pg. 83

What is the alternative to power religion? It is the religion of the Bible, which Martin Luther summarized as the "theology of the cross." Biblical religion is not a series of techniques for manipulating God's goodwill or harnessing God's power. Rather, it is a humble appeal for God's mercy and grace, which he has offered through the priestly ministry of his Son, Jesus Christ.

OBSERVING THE TEXT

3. What view do God's people seem to take of the ark of the covenant in 1 Samuel 4? How do the Philistines seem to view it in 1 Samuel 5? What is dangerously deficient and mistaken about both of their understandings?

4. What does the narrator want the reader to notice about the death of Eli? What makes his sad and despairing death such a low moment for the priesthood and the nation of Israel in general?

5. What does God demonstrate about his power, character, and rule throughout the events of 1 Samuel 5? How does this chapter serve to increase your understanding of his universal rule and his just punishment of unrepentant sin?

UNDERSTANDING THE TEXT

6. In what way do the Israelites seek to use the ark—as well as God himself—as a kind of good luck charm in their battle with the Philistines (4:1–5)? What is mistaken and misguided about their understanding of God?

7. What is the Philistines' response to the shouts that issue from God's people when the ark of the covenant enters the camp (4:7–11)? What might God be communicating to his people by allowing the ark to be captured by the Philistines?

8. How does the report that Eli receives in 4:12–18 echo the prophecies that he had heard both from the man of God and from Samuel? What news, in particular, seems most devastating to Eli (v. 18)? Why do you think this is?

9. What is significant about the name that Phinehas's widow gives to their son just before she dies (4:19–22)? How does this name capture the emptiness and despair of this moment in Israel's history?

Worldly Power over Religious Pretensions, pg. 82

This episode shows that when it comes to manipulating or exciting the carnal passions of men, the world is as adept as Christians, and even more able to muster worldly power. Unless our power in cultural and spiritual warfare is truly the might of God, directed by his Word, motivated by his grace, and animated by his Spirit, then the world's power is easily able to overcome our religious pretensions.

10. What do the Philistines seem to believe about their god Dagon—and about the God of Israel—based on what they do with the ark of the covenant (5:1–5)? What does God do to demonstrate how wrong they are? What are the Philistines shown about the identity and power of the God of Israel as a result of what happens to the idol Dagon?

11. How do the effects that the ark has on the Philistine towns of Ashdod and Gath illustrate the power of God? What is God teaching the Philistines through this experience? What might he be also teaching his own people about the ongoing love and care he has for them?

BIBLE CONNECTIONS

12. Read 1 Kings 18:20–40—another showdown that takes place between God and the false gods of the nations. How does God demonstrate his power and global rule in this passage from 1 Kings? What is similar between this passage and 1 Samuel 5?

13. The prophet Isaiah records this declaration from God: "I am God, and there is none like me" (Isa. 46:9). How does today's account from 1 Samuel demonstrate the uniqueness of the almighty God? What ought we to infer, from his absolute uniqueness, about the worship and obedience that we offer to him?

THEOLOGY CONNECTIONS

14. Answer 4 of the Westminster Shorter Catechism states that "God is a Spirit, infinite, eternal, and unchangeable, in his being, wisdom, power, holiness, justice, goodness, and truth." How might understanding and believing this description of God have helped the Israelites to avoid the mistaken thinking they displayed when they carried the ark into battle against the Philistines in 1 Samuel 4? How did their actions demonstrate that they had a shrunken view of God?

15. According to answer 26 of the Westminster Shorter Catechism, Christ executes the office he holds as king by "subduing us to himself, [by] ruling and defending us, and [by] restraining and conquering all his and our enemies." In what way do you see these "kingly" activities of Jesus Christ being demonstrated in your reading from 1 Samuel 4–5 today?

APPLYING THE TEXT

16. What would it look like if we, as Christians today, adopted the mindset that the Israelites had when they used the ark of the covenant? What fundamental misunderstandings about God, and about the way his power is to be used, can be seen both in 1 Samuel 4 as well as today?

17. What can the judgment that God's people experienced by suffering defeat at the hands of the Philistines teach us about our sin and God's justice? How do these realities point us to our need for Jesus and the cross?

18. How should the way that this reading portrayed Dagon "worshiping" Yahweh drive *you* to worship God more deeply today? What truths about his holiness, power, and glory should grip you as you study this passage?

God Is Not Overthrown, pg. 83
Whatever Israel and the Philistines might think, the capture of the ark and the defeat of Israel's army did not signify the overthrow of God. The elders thought that by bringing the ark they had ensured that God would defend his honor; little did they realize that God intended to defend his honor by sending the Philistines to bring judgment on his idolatrous people!

PRAYER PROMPT

As you close your study of this passage today, begin praying by actively repenting of your own tendency to use, control, or manipulate God for your own purposes as the Israelites did. Pray that he would give you a heart of humility that surrenders itself fully to his will, his Word, and his ways. Then ask him to remind you of the good purposes he has for his people. The creator God of the universe can never be defeated by the powers of this world; he will be glorified, he will win the battle, and he will accomplish his saving work for his helpless children.

LESSON 4

SAMUEL THE JUDGE

1 Samuel 6:1–7:17

THE BIG PICTURE

Our last lesson showed us quite a low point in the history of Israel. The Philistines captured the ark and routed the Israelites in battle. Eli, the high priest, died—and on the same day that his two wicked sons did, as well. A child was born and was named "Ichabod," out of despair, to commemorate the departing of the "glory of the Lord" from Israel. Yet that passage ended with a reminder that even though the Philistines had captured the ark, God had not been defeated. The Philistine god Dagon fell on his face in "worship" before the ark, whose presence wreaked havoc on the Philistines' towns!

In this lesson, you will see that the time has come for Samuel to take his place as the judge, priest, and prophet God has chosen for his people. The ark comes back to Israel after being sent off, with sacrifices and offerings, by the beleaguered Philistines (6:1–12). As the cows pull the cart containing the ark to the town of Beth-shemesh, its people rejoice and offer sacrifice and worship to God—only to witness his fierce judgment against many men from the town who look too closely upon the ark (6:13–20). So the ark is sent to Kiriath-jearim, where a priest is consecrated and set over its care (6:21–7:2). At this point, the ministry and rule of Samuel begins, and we see him judging God's people with godliness, truth, and integrity and calling them to repent and return to God in faith (7:3–17). The Lord brings surprising deliverance from the Philistines during the days of Samuel (vv. 10–11), and Samuel rules over Israel by taking regular

39

trips from town to town and proclaiming the words of God to the people (vv. 16–17). With this final, godly judge having now taken his place, God's people begin to turn back to him in obedience and worship—to forsake their idols and serve him alone.

Read 1 Samuel 6:1–7:17.

GETTING STARTED

1. In what ways are people today guilty of taking the holiness of God too lightly—whether with their words, through their actions, or even in their worship? In what ways have you yourself been guilty of this?

2. Are there times when you have renewed your commitment to the Lord—perhaps through fresh repentance, new humility, or a deeper commitment to the Word and prayer? What was the effect of a time when you renewed that commitment? What motivated it?

The Power to Turn from Sin, pg. 122
Single-minded devotion to the Lord requires forsaking false gods and turning from sin. But Samuel realized that the power for repentance comes from a new fervor for the Lord. We not only forsake the darkness but come to walk in the light. The power to turn from sin comes from seeing the glory of the Lord as the true God and the blessing of his salvation as our only true hope.

OBSERVING THE TEXT

3. What do you observe about the Philistines as they finally send the ark away from their towns (6:1–13)? What conclusion have they obviously drawn about the ark—and about the God who is attached to it?

4. What do God's people (and especially those in Beth-shemesh) still not seem to understand about his holiness? In what way does he demonstrate his holiness as well as his wrath in this passage?

5. How do you see Samuel emerging as a good and godly leader in 1 Samuel 7? What specific things does he do to help the people of Israel return to God? In what way is it evident that God is blessing Samuel's leadership?

UNDERSTANDING THE TEXT

6. How does the ark of God ultimately make its way back to Israel (6:1–12)? What role do the Israelites have in recapturing it? What might God be teaching his people, through this development, about their helplessness and his powerful might?

7. How do the people in the town of Beth-shemesh react when they receive the ark (6:13–16)? What goes terribly wrong in the way they treat the ark, though—and how does God respond to it (6:19–21)? What is more humble and appropriate about the way in which the residents of Kiriath-jearim respond to the ark and treat it as a symbol of God's presence with them (7:1–2)?

8. What is the initial effect of Samuel's leadership of the people of Israel (7:3–4)? What is their immediate response to his command? What makes a response like this so necessary—particularly during this time of the judges?

9. Describe the priestly role that Samuel played in the community of Israel (7:5–11). How do the specific actions and words that these verses describe put his spiritual guidance and leadership on display?

10. In what way does God respond to the intercessory prayer that Samuel offers for the people (7:10–11)? What brings about ongoing peace for God's people (7:12–14)? What do we learn from verses 15–17 about the ongoing roles Samuel held, and the activities he performed, as a prophet, priest, and judge for God's people?

11. In what way does Samuel point us in this passage to the priesthood and leadership of Jesus Christ? How do the roles that he embodies in this passage cause him to serve as a type of Jesus—our Priest, Prophet, and King?

The Role of the Ark, pg. 118

We have the benefit of God's completed revelation in the Old and New Testaments. This means not only that we can understand God's will simply by reading God's Word, but also that the story of redemption is now complete in the life and death of Jesus Christ. The ark played its role for a time, declaring God's holiness and mercy.

BIBLE CONNECTIONS

12. Review 1 Samuel 2:12–17—the passage that describes the sinful corruption of Eli's sons, who served as priests for God's people. In what ways does today's reading beautifully contrast the priestly leadership and ministry of Samuel with that of those evil men?

13. Hebrews 2:14–18 tells us about the beautiful and merciful high priestly ministry of Jesus Christ. Read those verses now. What hints of this priestly ministry of Jesus do you see being reflected by the leadership and priesthood of Samuel in the passage you have been studying?

BELIEVE IN JESUS - NOT IN OTHER GODS
THEY BOTH COMMITTED LIFE TO GOD -
(GREATEST HIGH PRIEST - JESUS) = DON'T NEED A
PRIEST TO GO
THRU

THEOLOGY CONNECTIONS

14. Samuel's ministry to and leadership over Israel begin with his call to the people to "return" to God with all their heart (7:3). The Westminster Confession of Faith describes repentance as involving a grief for and hatred of our sins, which cause us to turn from them and toward God (15.2). In what way does 1 Samuel 7 make it evident that Samuel is calling the people of Israel to this kind of repentance?

15. In the well-known 1758 hymn "Come, Thou Fount of Every Blessing," the hymnwriter Robert Robinson speaks of raising an "Ebenezer." How does 1 Samuel 7:12 deepen your understanding of the meaning of this word? What was Samuel doing—and calling the Israelites to do—by raising the "Ebenezer" stone?

SAMUEL OFFERED A WHOLE BURNT LAMB TO THE LORD (FOR ISRAEL)

— PHILISTINES GREW NEAR TO BATTLE ON ISRAEL & THE LORD THUNDERED LOUD — UPON THE PHILISTINES — SAMUEL TOOK STONE — CALLED IT EBENEZER

A MEMORIAL SET UP —

APPLYING THE TEXT

EBENEZER MEANING "HELP" — GOOD

16. What does today's reading call us to remember about the holiness of God and his infinite glory? In what ways have you perhaps taken him for granted or approached him flippantly or casually? What should you do in response to this?

17. How can the actions and leadership of Samuel serve to point us to the gentle and gracious way in which Jesus leads us? In what way has Jesus defeated your ultimate enemy? What has he done to serve as your ultimate sacrifice? How has he empowered you to live a life of obedience to God?

HE SHOWED THEM THAT THE HAND OF THE LORD WAS AGAINST THE PHILISTINES ALL THE DAYS OF SAMUEL —

THE Holy SPIRIT LIVES IN OUR HEART!

LOVE JOY PEACE

18. In what ways could we emulate the picture of repentance that we see in this passage—and particularly in 7:3–11? What blessings can we expect when we turn to God, humbly confess our sins, and put away idolatry in favor of serving him alone?

PRAYER PROMPT

As you conclude your study of this passage, consider the beautiful picture of renewal and repentance that it presents to Christians today. Pray that God would capture your heart with a vision of his holiness, glory, and power. Ask him to lead you toward right repentance as the Holy Spirit identifies within you areas of sin and opportunities for growth. Pray for your trust to be firmly planted in your Great High Priest, Jesus Christ, who gave himself for you and who leads you in the way of obedience to God.

A Return to God, pg. 127

Invigorated by God's mighty intervention, the Israelites sprang forward in new power. . . . What a difference this was from the weakness and despair of Israel at the beginning of the chapter! The Israelites returned to the Lord, confessed their sins, and appealed to God's grace in Christ with a sincere faith.

10-31-23

LESSON 5

A KING FOR ISRAEL
1 Samuel 8:1–11:15

THE BIG PICTURE

We have seen, in our previous lesson, the godly rule that Samuel instituted over God's people as their judge, priest, and prophet. Samuel speaks the words of God and calls God's people to repentance, and God honors him by granting his people victory over their enemies. As we will see in our lesson today, though, this is not enough for the people of Israel; they want a *king* to rule over them—and for all the wrong reasons!

The somewhat lengthy passage you will study today begins with the moral failure of Samuel's sons, which makes them unsuitable judges of Israel and leads the people to request a king like those of the nations around them (8:1–9)—a request that Samuel warns them about (8:10–22). We are then introduced to King Saul, through a winding narrative that begins with the case of his father's lost donkeys (9:1–10:16). Saul's search for the donkeys ultimately leads him to Samuel, who anoints him as the first king of Israel before sending him back home. When Saul is presented before the people of Israel, it is obvious that he looks the part in every way—he is tall, handsome, and kingly in appearance—and the people enthusiastically greet their new king (10:17–26). His reign begins with a display of godly restraint (10:27) as well as with a decisive and heroic military victory against the Ammonites, which brings relief to the people of Jabesh-gilead (11:1–11). The passage ends with the unification of the people of Israel under King Saul's rule (11:12–15). It is surely a strong start for this new

47

king—but we are left wondering whether Saul truly has the humble heart
of a godly king or merely *looks* the part.

Read 1 Samuel 8:1–11:15.

GETTING STARTED

1. What makes it dangerous for God's people, in any age, to seek to fit in
   with the world around them? What often motivates this desire we have
   to be more like the culture around us? How have you experienced this
   desire in your own heart and life?

   Human beings want to belong —
   Be true to yourself — Don't go along
   with the crowd —

2. Have you ever been caught up in the outward appearance of something—a person, product, or opportunity—that turned out to be mas-
   sively disappointing? Why are we so easily fooled by external beauty,
   charm, or strength?

A Rebellious Request, pg. 135
Their request represented a rebellion against God's rule; selfish in its
timing, since they demanded God's provision at the time of their own
choosing; and cowardly in its spirit, since they sought a system that
would remove the need for their faith in the Lord.

OBSERVING THE TEXT

3. What does the narrator seem to want us to notice throughout 1 Samuel 8 about the request that the elders and people of Israel make and about their motivation for making it? In what way do their words reveal their hearts? What do the words of God confirm about what the Israelites are after—and about why they want it?

4. What hints does this text from 1 Samuel offer—especially throughout chapters 9 and 10—about the character and heart of Saul? Do you sense any ominous clues that Saul may not be godly, humble, and strong in his heart and soul?

5. As chapter 10 concludes, what positive quality does Saul display (see v. 27)? In what way does 1 Samuel 11:1–15 portray a heroic beginning to his reign?

UNDERSTANDING THE TEXT

6. How does the failure of Samuel's sons that we see in 8:1–3 contribute to the request that the people make for a king—and in what way do these wicked sons echo previous passages we have seen in 1 Samuel? What else obviously lies behind the people's request for a king, and what explanation of the motivation behind their request does God offer to Samuel (8:5–9)?

7. How would you summarize the warnings that Samuel gives to the people of Israel regarding the king they are asking for (8:10–18)? What is their response to these warnings—and what is God's response to the people in turn (8:19–22)?

8. What evidence of God's sovereign direction do you see in the story of how Saul's pursuit of his lost donkeys leads him to meet Samuel (9:1–27)? How is Saul introduced to us in this chapter? What does the narrator want us to notice about him?

9. Describe the evidence you see in 1 Samuel 10:1–16 that God was involved in the calling and anointing of Saul. What seems to happen

to Saul spiritually after he meets Samuel and encounters the group of prophets (vv. 9–13)? What explanation might we offer of these spiritual experiences that occur in Saul's life?

10. What is surprising about Saul's behavior as Samuel prepares to introduce him to the people of Israel (10:20–22)? What does this potentially reveal about his character and heart? How does Samuel present Saul to the people—and how do they respond to their new king (10:23–24)?

11. How does Saul demonstrate godly restraint and humility in 10:27? What evidence of kingly valor and courage do you see in his initial actions, which he takes on behalf of the people of Jabesh-gilead (11:1–15)? Summarize your impressions of the beginning of King Saul's reign.

The King Who Gives, pg. 143–44

What a contrast there is between Jesus and the kings described by Samuel! Jesus is not a King who takes, but a King who gives. Jesus said, "The Son of Man came not to be served but to serve, and to give his life as a ransom for many" (Matt. 20:28). He gave his own life on the cross, dying in our place, that we might be freed from the guilt of our sin.

BIBLE CONNECTIONS

12. We know from Scripture that God anticipated what we see Israel doing in today's passage. Read Deuteronomy 17:14–20, which records the instructions Moses issues to God's people concerning their eventual kings. What are some of the things that Moses prohibits these kings from doing? How do these verses make it evident that a king of Israel should be a man of God's Word?

YOU MAY NOT SET A FOREIGNER OVER YOU, WHO IS NOT YOUR BROTHER —
HE SHALL NOT MULTIPLY HORSES FOR HIMSELF — NOR PEOPLE TO RTN TO EGYPT TO MULTIPLY HORSES & NOR (WIVES) OR SILVER OR GOLD — WRITE COPY LAW BE (ETC) READ FROM BIBLE

13. Read Ezekiel 25:1–7, which contains a prophecy against the Ammonites. What is the specific reason for the condemnation that God issues them through the prophet Ezekiel? What judgment is declared against them? In what way do the Ammonites in 1 Samuel 11 prove true to the way Ezekiel describes them in these verses?

A DEUT 17: 14-20

THEOLOGY CONNECTIONS

14. We saw in Deuteronomy 17 that God had precisely predicted that his people Israel would ask for a king so that they could be like the surrounding nations. In what way does this demonstrate his sovereignty and omniscience? And how does the selfish and sinful motivation that we see from Israel's elders also demonstrate the reality of human responsibility and sinful choice?

15. Question 26 of the Westminster Shorter Catechism describes the way in which Jesus serves as our King: "Christ executeth the office of a king, in subduing us to himself, in ruling and defending us, and in restraining and conquering all his and our enemies." Even though we can sense where Saul's reign is headed, in what way does the beginning of his rule provide at least a brief positive picture of the kingly reign of Christ Jesus that the catechism describes?

APPLYING THE TEXT

16. The Israelites are blatant and explicit about the motivation behind their desire for a king—it's so that they can be like "all the [other] nations" (8:5). In what way do your own thoughts, actions, or words perhaps betray the presence of this same motivation in your own heart?

17. What do you learn about God's character in this passage, as he gives the people what they ask for even though their motivation is sinful? In what way might he be disciplining his people by saying yes to them—and what could you learn from this?

18. How can the brief positive direction that King Saul's strong start takes paint a picture of Jesus's own reign and the deliverance he has won for you? In what way does the gracious restraint that Saul shows toward his enemies serve as a picture of the grace Jesus shows toward you? What beautiful connection with Christ's salvation do you see in Saul's rescue of the helpless people of Jabesh-gilead?

PRAYER PROMPT

Like the people of Israel who looked to a handsome king who would help them to be "like . . . the nations," we too are drawn toward fitting in rather than standing out as courageous followers of Jesus Christ! As you close your study of this passage from 1 Samuel, begin praying by confessing to God your tendency to be drawn toward seeking friendship with the world and to be caught up in outward appearances. Ask God to give you faith in his Son—our true King. Praise Jesus for humbly giving himself for you and for leading you in victory against Satan, sin, and even death itself.

We Need a Savior, pg. 179
This chapter presents the theme of salvation in Israel, and thus reminds us that God's people need a Savior to deliver us. . . . Realizing this, we should draw near to the true Spirit-empowered King whom God has sent into our world.

LESSON 6

FROM SAMUEL TO SAUL

1 Samuel 12:1–14:23

THE BIG PICTURE

In our last lesson, we considered the sinful request from God's people to have a king so that they can be "like all the nations" (8:5). Despite stern warnings from Samuel, they continue to demand a king; and so God gives them Saul who looks the part in every way. Saul starts his reign well, demonstrating restraint toward his local enemies and bringing valiant military rescue to the helpless residents of the nearby Jabesh-gilead, who are being ravaged by the Ammonites (10:27–11:15). But, sadly, Saul's reign takes a sharp downward turn from there.

Today you will read and study the farewell address that Samuel delivers to Israel, which describes the fickle history of the faith they have shown God during the period of the judges as well as Samuel's own steady, faithful leadership and prophetic ministry (12:1–25). His ominous words of warning that conclude chapter 12 give way to the first major act of disobedience by Israel's new king (13:1–15). In advance of a battle against the Philistines, King Saul disobeys a clear instruction from Samuel to wait until he arrives to offer a sacrifice to God; instead he offers the sacrifice himself, unlawfully carrying out the office of the priest, which brings him stern rebuke from Samuel (vv. 13–14). From 13:16–14:23, the people continue to fight against the Philistines under the leadership of their failed king—whose son Jonathan emerges as both a brave and a heroic figure. God gives a great victory into the hands of the Israelites, even as the shadow of Saul's sin continues to hang over the narrative. We are left with this question: will God's hand of blessing remain on this king who will not live under his commands?

Read 1 Samuel 12:1–14:23

GETTING STARTED

1. What spiritual truths do you tend to forget most easily? In what ways and for what reasons do you tend to fall prey to "spiritual amnesia"—and when this happens, what do you do in order to actively remember the truths of God's love, his gospel, and his grace?

2. When do hurry, busyness, or stress tend to get in the way of your spending time with God—either through prayer or through studying his Word on your own or with others? What excuses do you sometimes use in order to justify this?

A New Focus, pg. 192
With these words, the narrative of 1 Samuel transitions from its focus on Samuel to a new focus on King Saul. Samuel had been a faithful servant of the Lord, as the people attested, and a truly great man of God.

OBSERVING THE TEXT

3. As Samuel comes to the end of his time as the leader of Israel, what does the speech that he gives in chapter 12 make it seem is his greatest concern regarding the people of God? In what way do his words affirm his godliness, his faithfulness, and the concern that he has for Israel's holiness and their obedience to their God?

4. What character traits of Saul begin to emerge in chapter 13? What is so troubling about the decisions he makes—and about the way he responds when he is confronted by Samuel?

5. How does the narrator introduce us to Jonathan, the son of Saul? What role does he begin to play in the narrative—and what hints do we get of his future importance to the story?

UNDERSTANDING THE TEXT

6. In what ways does Samuel seek to vindicate his own ministry and leadership (12:1–5)? What does he say to set the people's evil request for a king within the broader context of the sin they have committed during the time of the judges (12:6–17)?

7. What response do the people give to Samuel's words—and in what way does he intercede for them (12:18–23)? With what words of warning does Samuel conclude—and what makes these feel like slightly ominous words as King Saul's reign begins (12:24–25)?

8. Why is Saul's presumptuous action of making the sacrifice himself so sinful and rebellious (13:8–9)? What happens in the context of these verses that might have caused him to make this decision?

SAMUEL GAVE SAUL ISTRUCTIONS TO WAIT
TILL SAMUEL ARRIVED BEFORE MAKING
THE SACRIFICE.

> **More Important Than Survival, pg. 201**
> The sacrifices Saul desecrated were holy, and they dealt with holy things, such as God's wrath against our sin and his atoning work in Christ for our forgiveness. Objectively, it was more important for God to be worshiped properly than for Israel to survive its war.

9. How does Samuel respond to Saul's unlawful sacrifice (13:11–15)?
   What, according to him, will be the consequences of Saul's actions?
   What kind of king is God already seeking out to lead his people—and
   how does this description foreshadow a different anointed king whom
   we will soon meet (v. 14)?

10. Describe the plight and the military status of the Israelites, according
    to 13:16–23. What advantages do the Philistines have over them?

11. In what way does Jonathan demonstrate bravery and courage in battle
    (14:1–14)? What do we learn about his character from these verses?
    How does his courageous fight spur on a surprising victory for the
    Israelites against the Philistines (14:15–23)?

BIBLE CONNECTIONS

12. Read Genesis 14:17–20, which records the meeting between Abram
    and Melchizedek. What two roles does this passage appear to portray
    Melchizedek holding?

13. Now read Psalm 110:1–4 and Hebrews 7:11–17. In what ways do both David and the author of Hebrews portray Jesus as being a priest after the "order" of Melchizedek? Why is it possible for Jesus to be both a King (who is from the tribe of Judah) and a Priest, according to Hebrews 7:14–16? What additional light do these passages shed on the arrogant and presumptuous sin that King Saul commits in 1 Samuel 13?

THEOLOGY CONNECTIONS

14. The people of Israel cry to Samuel in 12:19 for mediation; they plea for him to pray to God on their behalf so that God will show them mercy and grace. The Westminster Confession of Faith speaks of Christ's mediating role this way: "The Godhead and the manhood . . . were inseparably joined together in one person, without conversion, composition, or confusion. Which person is very God and very man, yet one Christ, the only mediator between God and man" (8.2). What makes Jesus Christ absolutely unique as well as worthy of being the ultimate Mediator between us and God?

15. John Calvin asserts, while writing about the role that God played in Saul's life, that "when he was pleased to set Saul over the kingdom, he made him as it were a new man" (*Institutes*, 2.3.4). What theological difficulties does Saul's disobedience, and God's subsequent rejection of him as king, raise for us? How can the rest of Scripture (see, for

instance, Heb. 6:4–6) inform our understanding of Saul's life, his faith, and his rejection of God's rule?

APPLYING THE TEXT

16. Which of Samuel's stern commands and warnings in 12:24–25 should you seek to apply to your spiritual life today? What makes you tend to forget, at times, the "great things he has done for you"?

17. In what ways are you sometimes tempted, like Saul, to sin because of impatience, expediency, or convenience? How can you discipline your heart to be patient, to worship, and to obey Scripture—even when doing so is difficult?

Our King Reigns and Reconciles, pg. 205
Jesus' success as the man after God's own heart means that *we have a king who reigns secure from an eternal throne.* . . . Furthermore, through Jesus' righteousness *we have a Mediator who reconciles the fallen children of Adam through his own perfect obedience.*

18. How does the failure that Saul exhibited as both a king and a priest for God's people point us, by contrast, to the perfect way that Jesus reigns over and ministers to us as our eternal King and Great High Priest? What makes it such good news that your Savior both rules over you and mediates for you?

PRAYER PROMPT

As you close your study of this lesson today, spend some time praising God for the gift of Jesus Christ. He is a better mediator than Samuel, a better king than Saul, and the great eternal High Priest of sinners who are in need of God's mercy. Ask God to give you a humble and obedient heart so that you will be more concerned with rightly worshiping him than with expediency, worldly success, or even safety and comfort. Confess to him the ways in which you, like Saul, are tempted to be impatient and to prioritize convenience rather than patiently obeying what God says.

LESSON 7

SAUL'S DESCENT

1 Samuel 14:24–15:35

THE BIG PICTURE

After the reign of King Saul got off to a strong start, our last lesson showed us how he failed to listen to the instructions of Samuel—and to submit to the words of God. Following the unlawful sacrifice that Saul offered, God spoke of the man "after his own heart" whom he would raise up to be a godly king over his people. We were also introduced to Jonathan, the courageous warrior son of Saul. Our passage for today begins with him.

After Saul makes a rash and foolish vow that promises death to anyone who eats before the Philistines have been defeated (14:24), Jonathan and his men strengthen themselves with honey in preparation for battle (14:25–30). This ultimately leads to a confrontation with Saul, who seems ready to fulfill his vow by having his own son put to death (14:31–44). His own men rise up against him to deliver Jonathan from death, providing an early demonstration of Saul's failure in the areas of wisdom and leadership (14:45–52). And in chapter 15, Saul's descent continues: he goes from being *rash* in his vow to *resistant* to full obedience to God. The Lord gives him a clear command, through Samuel, to attack the Amalekites and make a complete end of them (15:1–3). Saul does attack . . . but he leaves King Agag and the best of the livestock alive (15:4–9). When he is confronted by Samuel, Saul does everything but admit his guilt: he claims ignorance and blames his soldiers for the sin before finally asking Samuel to pray to God for his forgiveness (15:10–25). This confrontation between Saul and

63

Samuel ends with Samuel's robe ripping away in Saul's grasping hand—a picture that Samuel uses as a symbol of how God will tear the kingdom out of Saul's grasp in order to give it to another (15:26–28). As the chapter concludes, it is Samuel who fulfills God's command by executing the Amalekite king and thereby obediently carrying out the command of God that Saul was unwilling to fulfill (15:29–35). We can see clearly now that God's people need a better king than Saul.

Read 1 Samuel 14:24–15:35.

GETTING STARTED

1. How have rash decisions, words, or promises harmed you—or others whom you know? Why do we sometimes tend to make impulsive and foolish decisions, and what can we do to guard ourselves against such folly?

2. What excuses have you made for the times when you have not completely obeyed God's Word on a certain point? What outside influences have you been tempted to blame—friends, culture, stress, and so on—for your own sinful choices or actions?

Folly and Downfall, pg. 226

Modern examples of calamitous folly and precipitous fall . . . pale in comparison to the folly and fall of Israel's King Saul. His willful sin had resulted in his rejection by the Lord (1 Sam. 13:13–14). Now, his willful folly had resulted in his fall from any hold on credibility as the leader over his nation, even while Saul remained enthroned as king.

OBSERVING THE TEXT

3. Note the words, behavior, and decisions that Saul engages in throughout 1 Samuel 14. What makes it obvious that he is acting foolishly and impulsively? What might be the motivations behind the rash vow he makes? How do his men respond to this?

4. In what ways does Saul persist in being disobedient throughout 1 Samuel 15? How does Samuel respond to him—and why does he take Saul's disobedience so seriously?

5. How does God communicate to Saul throughout this passage? What seems to grieve him the most about Saul's behavior? What do you learn about the character of God throughout this passage?

UNDERSTANDING THE TEXT

6. What makes Saul's vow in 14:24 so rash and foolish? What might have motivated him to make this vow? What further light do Jonathan's words in 14:29–30 shed on the foolish impulsiveness of Saul's vow—and of the harm that it brought to God's people?

7. How do the people step in to defend Jonathan from death at the hand of his father (14:43–46)? How does this serve as an indication of their lack of respect for King Saul? What are we seeing happen to his credibility and authority?

8. What are the clear instructions that Samuel gives to Saul regarding his battle against the Amalekites (15:1–3)? Is there any room for Saul to misinterpret this command? Why, or why not? What does this command reveal about the holy character of God and the wrath he has against sin?

The Failure of Fearful Leaders, pg. 238
Saul was cut from the same cloth as Aaron and many other failed leaders who did not obey the Lord because they feared the scorn of the people. Saul would have honored God in obedience only if he had forbidden the people to take the Amalekites' sheep and oxen and insisted that all things be done in accordance with God's actual commands.

9. In what specific ways does Saul disobey God's command (15:4–9)? What is God's response to this? What is Samuel's (15:10–11)?

10. How does Saul seek to minimize his own sin and disobedience throughout 15:13–21? What does Samuel explain to Saul that God truly wants from him above all else (15:22–23)?

11. What does 15:24–29 say will eventually result from Saul's intentional disobedience to the commands of God? What part of this exchange between Samuel and Saul hints that a better king is coming for God's people? What does Samuel ultimately do to fulfill God's righteous judgment against his enemies (15:32–33)?

BIBLE CONNECTIONS

12. One of the difficult aspects of this passage is God's command for Saul to utterly annihilate the Amalekites—their people, king, livestock, and possessions. It is important to understand that hundreds of years of history lie behind this command. Read Exodus 17:8–16 and then

Deuteronomy 25:17–19. What do these passages contribute to our understanding of the sin the Amalekites had committed against both God and his people?

13. God rejects King Saul because of his disobedience—his rebellious failure to submit to God's commands. Read Hebrews 5:7–10. What does this passage teach us about the perfect obedience of Jesus Christ, our Savior? How does Christ the King serve as a stark contrast to King Saul?

THEOLOGY CONNECTIONS

14. It is extremely important to understand the difference between Israel under the old covenant (when it was ruled directly by God) and the nations of which we are citizens today. Christians belong to the new covenant people of God—the church—and, as Richard Phillips states, "The only arena in which God's people today practice holy war is spiritual warfare."[1] What is important about this distinction between the old covenant and new covenant people of God? How could this distinction prove helpful when you are having conversations about the Bible with unbelievers?

1. Richard D. Phillips, *1 Samuel*, Reformed Expository Commentary (Phillipsburg, NJ: 2012), 231.

15. Saul was commanded to execute God's righteous judgment against the sinful Amalekites—but he completely failed to do so. There will come a day, though, when God's perfect King executes his final judgment on all creation. As the Westminster Confession of Faith puts it, "God hath appointed a day wherein he will judge the world in righteousness by Jesus Christ, to whom all power and judgment is given of the Father" (33.1). What should make this truth encouraging for believers in Jesus Christ—and frightening for those who do not know him?

APPLYING THE TEXT

16. Describe times when you have hurt others through your impulsive decisions or rash words. How could you seek, by God's grace, to humbly make this right?

17. In what ways should 1 Samuel 15, and especially the excuses that it shows Saul making as well as his dismissal of his sin, convict you of your own tendencies to only partially obey God's Word? In what areas of your life might God be calling you to obey him more fully?

18. How can this passage's portrayal of King Saul serve as a contrast with Jesus—a contrast that helps to strengthen your confidence in him? What makes the perfect righteousness and obedience of Jesus such good news for *you*, personally?

PRAYER PROMPT

As you consider the sad and sinful descent of King Saul, a good thing for you to pray is that God would use this account to serve as a warning to your own life and heart. Ask him to protect you from indulging in sinful impulses and rash behaviors. Pray that he would guard your heart from caring more about the opinions of others than about the power and authority of his Word. And pray, too, that this passage would drive you to the perfect King, whose perfect obedience to the Father was part of what made his death on the cross effective for you. Pray that Jesus Christ will rule over your heart as you seek, in his strength, to obey your heavenly Father.

Accomplishing the Work, pg. 240
The ultimate contrast with Saul is the true King of God's people, the righteous Lord Jesus Christ. When Jesus presented himself to God at the end of his earthly ministry, he could give a report very different from King Saul's. Jesus prayed to the Father, "I glorified you on earth, having accomplished the work that you gave me to do" (John 17:4).

JAN 9

LESSON 8

THE ANOINTED KING

1 Samuel 16:1–23

THE BIG PICTURE

In the midst of King Saul's descent, God accompanied his rebuke of the king with a promise that he made to his people: namely, that he would give them another king, who would be a man after his own heart (13:14). In this lesson, we meet the unlikely next king of Israel: the humble shepherd boy David. At the beginning of 1 Samuel 16, we come to a transition point—while the story of King Saul's reign will continue, it is David who will emerge as the focal point of the narrative from here onward.

In this chapter, God directs Samuel to anoint the next king of Israel, whom he identifies as one of the sons of a man from Bethlehem named Jesse (16:1). So Samuel arranges to meet Jesse and his sons by inviting them to attend a sacrifice of worship that he is leading (16:2–5). Handsome son after handsome son passes before Samuel—and yet God selects none of them (16:6–10). Even this godly prophet needs to be reminded of one of the central truths of 1 Samuel: "Man looks on the outward appearance, but the LORD looks on the heart" (v. 7). Ultimately, it is Jesse's youngest son, David, who is chosen by God and anointed by Samuel to be the next king of Israel (16:11–13). Young David, a skilled harpist, is eventually taken into the service of King Saul so that he can offer soothing music to calm Saul's frequent spiritual attacks (16:14–23).

This passage highlights the sovereign and loving care that God shows to the people of Israel by providing for them, after Saul's failure, a godly king after his own heart. It also points us forward to the unlikely King and humble Savior of God's people—who will, himself, be born in Bethlehem.

Read 1 Samuel 16:1–23.

GETTING STARTED

1. What are some of the characteristics of a great and godly leader? Whom have you seen demonstrating those characteristics well, and how? Where would humility rank on your priority list of traits that characterize a good leader?

2. In what ways have you been guilty of focusing too much on outward appearances? Why is it so difficult for us to remember that God does not look at outward appearances but considers the hearts of men and women?

The Coming King, pg. 255

Chapter 16 marks a major transition in the books of Samuel, but more than that, it begins one of the most extraordinary accounts in all the Bible or any other literature. The coming of David has been alluded to earlier in Samuel, but now the sacred text turns directly to the story of Israel's great champion, poet, prophet, and king.

OBSERVING THE TEXT

3. Look back to 1 Samuel 9:1–2 and 10:23–24 and note the descriptions that these passages contain of King Saul. What does the narrator seek to highlight about Saul? How does this impact the way we should think about the sons of Jesse?

4. What mistaken way of thinking does even Samuel demonstrate in this chapter, thereby showing that he needs God's correction? How does God gently correct him and teach him about the perspective he takes on human beings (16:7)?

5. What does the narrator reveal to us about David as he first introduces us to him? In what way does David differ from Saul? What is ironic and surprising about what happens in the second part of the chapter (16:14–23)?

UNDERSTANDING THE TEXT

6. What initial objection does Samuel offer regarding God's command for him to go to Bethlehem where Jesse is—and how does he end up disguising his true purpose (16:1–5)?

7. What initial evaluation does Samuel seem to make about the sons of Jesse as they parade before him (16:6–10)? What does God remind Samuel about the perspective that he takes on humanity (v. 7)—and how could you interpret this as a key theme of the book of 1 Samuel, based on what you have studied from it thus far (16:7)?

8. Note the initial words that David's father Jesse speaks about him, as well as the initial description he is given in the text (16:11–12). What does Jesse seem to imply about his youngest son? How does what he implies differ from the opinion of David that God holds? What happens in 16:13 as Samuel anoints David—and where have we seen this before?

9. In what way does the anointing of young David point us forward to the coming of God's own Son, Jesus Christ? How do we see David serving as an Old-Testament *type* of Jesus Christ in this passage?

The Greatest and Clearest, pg. 265

The anointing of David marked a significant advance in God's redeeming plan for history. Moreover, it pointed forward to the greatest advancement in God's salvation, which would come with the entry of his own Son, Jesus Christ. Of all the types of Christ in the Old Testament . . . David is the greatest and clearest.

10. Describe the torment that Saul experiences, along with what seems to be the reason that it afflicts his life (16:14–15). What remedy do his servants suggest (16:16–18)? What skill of David's do we learn about in this passage?

11. What is ironic and surprising about the way in which Saul responds to David (16:21–23)? In what way can you see this response fitting into God's sovereign plan for his servant David—as well as for his people overall?

BIBLE CONNECTIONS

12. In 1 Corinthians 1:26–27, Paul writes of the way in which God uses what is "foolish" in the eyes of the world to shame what the world considers to be "wise." Read those verses now. In what way do 1 Samuel 16 and the anointing of David illustrate the gospel principle that Paul explains here?

13. As God withdraws his Spirit from King Saul, he also allows Saul to be tormented by a harmful spirit. Read Zechariah 1:3. What wise prophetic counsel could this verse have offered to King Saul at this point in his life?

THEOLOGY CONNECTIONS

14. Seeing God elect and anoint David to be the next king reminds us of how, in his sovereign and free will, he has called all his children to himself. God doesn't look on David's appearance or reputation but chooses his king for his own purposes and his own reasons. Why is it good news for sinners that God elects to save us regardless of our appearance or reputation?

15. Answer 27 of the Heidelberg Catechism explains that God, in his providence, "upholds heaven, earth, and all creatures, and so governs them that herbs and grass, rain and drought, fruitful and barren years, food and drink, health and sickness, riches and poverty, yea, all things, come not by chance but by His fatherly hand." How does this truth help us to understand the role that God played in the way that David has been brought into the service of King Saul—who will eventually become his enemy . . . and even attempt to kill him?

APPLYING THE TEXT

16. What might have happened if Samuel had anointed one of Jesse's handsome, strong elder sons to be the next king of Israel? How does this passage shake your confidence in the wisdom of the world and strengthen your confidence in God's wisdom, which is revealed in the gospel of his Son?

17. What is encouraging to you about what God says in 1 Samuel 16:7? In what way should his words convict and challenge you?

18. What does God's providential plan to bring David into the service of Saul (and thus to prepare him for his next step toward kingship) teach you about how his sovereign work and care manifests itself in your life? What do you need to remember, today, about his often mysterious purposes for your life?

PRAYER PROMPT

Ultimately this passage should lead you to praise the humble and gracious King and Savior of God's people: Jesus Christ. He took on our humanity, bore our flesh, carried our sins, and is now exalted as the risen and reigning Lord of all! Today, praise God for the gift of his Anointed One, who came to earth in God's perfect timing to bring salvation to sinners who look to him in faith. Pray to God, as well, that you would be able to emulate David, who humbly served Saul, waited on the Lord, and faithfully prepared himself for all that God had planned for him.

Part of God's Plan, pg. 268
As David entered into Saul's service as court musician, the youth may not have understood how or why this was happening. But David could be sure that this summons had arrived for a reason, since God's gracious purposes always guide the events of his people's lives.

LESSON 9

A CHAMPION FOR ISRAEL

1 Samuel 17:1–18:5

THE BIG PICTURE

In 1 Samuel 16, God's chosen king—the man after "his own heart"—was anointed by Samuel. David was truly an unlikely king—he was a shepherd boy, the youngest of all of Jesse's strong and handsome sons, and seemingly overlooked by everyone. Yet God saw David's heart, and he chose him to be Israel's next king.

Now, in 1 Samuel 17, the anointed king reveals his courageous heart—as well as his zeal for the glory and honor of the Lord God. It should be noted that you are studying one of the most well-known accounts in all of Scripture today—and yet it is also a passage that is notorious for the way in which it is moralized and analogized (for example, many people have used this passage to teach Christians about fighting "giants"—or, in other words, problems—in their lives). When we understand it in the broader context of 1 Samuel and all of Scripture, we see within this account a great picture of God's anointed king doing battle on behalf of his helpless people—and all for the glory of God's name.

As the passage begins, King Saul finds himself in great trouble—a Philistine giant is challenging Israel to provide a champion to engage in representative warfare (17:1–11). While all of Israel quakes in fear at Goliath and his challenge, God ordains for young David to arrive in the camp at just the right time to witness the mocking words of Goliath (17:12–30). Despite the jeers of his older brother, David speaks angrily and courageously about Goliath—and what he says is reported to King Saul, who summons him and attempts to clothe him for battle (17:31–40). David runs to battle against Goliath armed with only a sling and five smooth stones (17:41–45), but he declares with courage that God will give him the victory so that "all the earth may know that there is a God in Israel" (17:46). David topples Goliath with a stone from his sling—and then beheads the giant with his own sword (17:47–51). In response to this, the Israelites chase down their enemies with a shout as David grows in favor with them as well as with Saul and Jonathan (17:52–18:5). The anointed king has proved his worth—and it is clear that David is the right man to lead and save Israel.

Read 1 Samuel 17:1–18:5.

GETTING STARTED

1. What obstacles have you encountered in your life that have seemed insurmountable? How did you respond to them? To what extent were praying and seeking God's guidance involved in your response?

Foreshadowed Victory, pg. 279

As we approach this great chapter, we should realize that David's victory does not primarily foretell triumphs that we will achieve by faith but rather the victory of Christ for our salvation. David as hero and king presents a foreshadowing portrait—what theologians refer to as a *type*—of his greater Son, Jesus.

2. How have you heard the story of David and Goliath being applied to Christians today—whether in Sunday school lessons, in sermons, or in Christian literature or music? In general, when this story is told, with which character is the audience asked to identify?

OBSERVING THE TEXT

3. Look back briefly at 1 Samuel 16 and consider the way in which young David is contrasted with his older brothers (even by Samuel!). Why might people not have expected young David to amount to much on the battlefield?

4. Note what Goliath says in 1 Samuel 17—and then contrast his words with what David says in verses 41–47. What is very different about the way they both speak about the God of Israel?

5. What do we see Saul doing throughout this passage? Whom might we *expect* to serve as the champion of Israel and to go out and fight Goliath? How does this chapter serve to further develop the ways in which Saul has failed as a leader, a man of God, and a man of courage?

UNDERSTANDING THE TEXT

6. How does the narrator describe the Philistine champion, Goliath—
   and what details does he choose to include in his description of him
   (17:4–10)? What do you notice about Goliath's words? How does the
   Israelite army respond to his challenge (17:11)?

7. What do we continue to learn in 1 Samuel 17:12–30 about David's godly
   and courageous character? What seems to excite his anger the most?
   How does his older brother respond to him—and in what way does
   this continue chapter 16's theme of how man looks on the "outward
   appearance" while God looks at the "heart"?

8. Note the way that Saul responds to David's bold and courageous words
   as well as the way that he "arms" him for battle (17:31–40). What is so
   surprising about the way that David ultimately sets out to do combat
   with the Philistine champion? How is the message of 1 Samuel 16:7
   demonstrated through the contrast between the way that David prepares for battle and the way that Goliath does (17:4–7)?

9. As the men of Israel stand frightened on the sidelines, the young
   anointed one quickly runs to engage in battle against their brutal enemy
   (17:48). What does David value most, according to what he says to

Goliath—and what does he hope will result from his victory over the giant (17:45–47)? In what way does David's victory over Goliath present a picture of the greater victory that Jesus Christ won over Satan, sin, and death (17:48–50)?

10. Describe what happens to the Philistines and the Israelites after Goliath falls dead (17:51–54). How do verses 52 and 53 also remind us of the victory Christ won for his people on the cross as we see the previously helpless soldiers of Israel now chasing down their enemies with a shout?

11. What is Saul's response to David's victorious battle against Goliath (17:55–18:2)? What happens between David and Saul's son, Jonathan; and what does Jonathan indicate about his understanding of the purpose God has for David through the gifts that he gives to him (18:1–4)? In what way do the people respond to David in verse 5—and what encourages us to interpret all of these responses to David's victory as being evidence of God's sovereign hand in his life?

A Picture of Our Deliverance, pg. 302

We cannot reflect on David's heroism without realizing that his example points us forward to the coming of God's true champion, the royal Savior of the house of David, God's son, Jesus Christ. From the earliest days of the church, God's people have seen David's victory over Goliath as a picture of our deliverance from Satan and the bonds of sin and hell.

BIBLE CONNECTIONS

12. Read Colossians 2:13–15, which beautifully describes the salvation that Christ secured through the cross as well as the triumph he won over Satan and his evil servants. In what way does David put God's enemies to "open shame" in 1 Samuel 17—and how do you see this serving as an intentional foretaste of Jesus's victory on the cross?

13. Paul writes in Ephesians 6:13–17 about putting on the full "armor of God." Read those verses now. What makes it evident that David puts on the "armor of God" even though he discards Saul's armor? What could you do to actively put on the spiritual armor that Paul describes?

THEOLOGY CONNECTIONS

14. One of the key doctrines of the Reformed faith is that our salvation is a *monergistic* act of God rather than a *synergistic* act of cooperation between us and God. In other words, sinners are justified by God's grace *alone*—not by a cooperation between God's grace and their *good works*. How does the victory that David won against Goliath on behalf of the helpless Israel serve as a vivid illustration of this theological doctrine?

15. The often-repeated answer to the first question of the Westminster Shorter Catechism is that the chief end of man is "to glorify God and to enjoy him forever." How does 17:46–47 make it evident that David's chief motivation for fighting Goliath is the glory of God, rather than earthly reward or even a military victory for Israel?

APPLYING THE TEXT

16. What should the picture that 1 Samuel 17 presents of Saul and the Israelites teach you about your sin, weakness, and helplessness? In what way are we meant to see our own need for Jesus as we observe these men quaking in fear at the feet of the mighty Philistine giant?

17. What do you see in this passage that can help to make the gospel of Jesus Christ even more beautiful to you? In what way can David's passion and zeal for God's glory serve as an example of the way that you too should desire the exaltation of God's name throughout the earth?

A Giving Love, pg. 320–21

Jonathan's was not only a love that rejoiced, but also a love that gave. What a remarkable scene it was when Israel's prince and captain approached David after his victory and "stripped himself of the robe that was on him and gave it to David, and his armor, and even his sword and his bow and his belt" (1 Sam. 18:4).

18. What model does Jonathan offer to us of the right response we should have to Jesus Christ—the King and Savior of God's people? How should the sacrificial gifts that he gives to David shape the humble and sacrificial devotion that we give to Jesus as we seek his glory instead of our own?

PRAYER PROMPT

The account of David's victory over Goliath ought to make us rejoice at the salvation God has won for us through Jesus Christ, the Anointed One. As you close your study of this passage, praise God that he provided salvation through Jesus for you—even as you stood helplessly on the sidelines because of your sin! Thank him for a King and Savior who is greater than David and who defeated your greatest enemies—Satan, sin, and death—through his death and resurrection. Then pray to be able to respond to Jesus the way Jonathan responded to David: with rejoicing, humility, and sacrificial giving and service.

LESSON 10

ENEMIES AND FRIENDS

1 Samuel 18:6–20:42

THE BIG PICTURE

First Samuel 17 has brought us to a high point in the book's narrative, as the young anointed one David has achieved victory for Israel over the enemy champion Goliath. God's chosen king has proven his worth through the zeal he has displayed for God's glory and the representative victory he has won for God's people. Yet David will now experience a long period of suffering and trial that will precede his exaltation to the throne of Israel—a period that we will see beginning in our lesson for today.

As David enters the service of Saul, he is surrounded by the love and adulation of the people of Israel, who sing songs in his honor that celebrate his military victories (18:6–7). This almost immediately leads Saul to nurse a growing envy and hatred of David in his heart as he begins to view him as a rival and a threat to his power and rule (18:8–9). After making an unsuccessful attempt on David's life in a fit of rage (18:10–11), Saul devises a plan to send him out to battle and then to arrange for him to be killed at the hands of the Philistines by promising his daughter Michal to David in marriage for the price of one hundred dead Philistines (18:12–30). This attempt is unsuccessful as well, as David slays two hundred Philistines and continues to win the admiration and respect of all Israel. In the next chapter, Saul seeks to enlist the help of his own family members in order to destroy David, only to find that both Jonathan and Michal are loyal to his new son-in-law. Jonathan refuses to kill David, and he makes Saul promise not to harm him either (19:1–7). Saul's daughter Michal arranges for David to escape from Saul's men—which ultimately leads to King Saul's humilia-tion by the Spirit of God (19:8–24). Jonathan and David strengthen their friendship in 1 Samuel 20 by making a covenant, through which the son of King Saul humbly supports God's anointed one—even though doing so will mean his own abdication of the throne (20:1–42). Even through danger and trial, God is preserving his anointed one—and preparing him to lead his people Israel.

Read 1 Samuel 18:6–20:42.

GETTING STARTED

1. What situations or occurrences that you have encountered have made you feel the most insecure? In those instances, have you also struggled with feeling envious of others—and why?

2. In what ways has God used seasons of trial or testing in your life to prepare you for new callings or endeavors? What was most difficult for you while you were in the *midst* of those seasons? What changed regarding the perspective you took on those trials as you looked *back* on them and saw God's hand in them?

OBSERVING THE TEXT

3. Notice how Saul's attitude regarding David quickly changes as this passage begins (and contrast this attitude with the one we saw in 1 Samuel 18:1–5). What seems to prompt this change in his perception of David? What does he fear? What might be causing his fear to turn to anger and violence?

4. Consider the ways in which Jonathan, Michal, and the people of Israel respond to David throughout this passage. How do the attitudes and actions of these characters contrast with Saul's?

5. What are these chapters teaching us about David's character? How does he respond to others throughout the events that they describe?

Trial and Testing, pg. 326
This episode begins a long period of trouble and hardship for young David. It may be ironic that hatred for David appeared immediately after his great [military] achievement . . . and his sudden elevation to prominence, but it is not coincidental. We can see in David's long period of trial and testing . . . the hand of God in preparing his servant.

UNDERSTANDING THE TEXT

6. How do the people of Israel respond to David's military victories—
   and what might have made their songs particularly painful for King
   Saul (18:6–7)? What attitudes and actions of Saul's does the narrator
   describe in 18:8–15?

7. What is Saul's deceitful plan regarding David—and in what way does
   David's humility help him (18:17–19)? How does Saul seek to use
   his daughter Michael, as well as the enemy Philistines, to bring about
   David's downfall (18:20–30)? In what ways does this section make it
   evident that God's hand of blessing is upon David's life?

8. How does Jonathan begin to act as an advocate for David (19:1–7)? In
   what way do we see Saul's murderous hatred rising up again, however,
   in 19:8–10? What does Michal do to side with David against her father
   Saul's murderous pursuit of him (19:11–17)?

9. What is surprising and ironic about what happens to Saul when he pursues David to Ramah (19:18–24)? What might God be communicating to Saul about himself through this—as well as about his sinful and murderous pursuit of David?

10. Describe the agreement that David and Jonathan come to in order to confirm what Saul's true intentions are regarding David (20:1–23). In what way does Saul demonstrate his murderous rage and erase all doubt about his intentions for David (20:24–34)?

11. What behavior does Jonathan exhibit toward his father (20:34) and toward David (20:35–42)? How do you see him continuing to model the right response to the Lord's anointed one? What does the Lord seem to have in store for David before the time that he will bring him to the throne?

The Blessing of Humility, pg. 333
This passage reveals the third person who is present—the One whose actions dominate this chapter. We have considered Saul as a classic picture of the mad anxiety that accompanies life without God. David, on the other hand, demonstrates the humility that leads to God's protection and blessing.

BIBLE CONNECTIONS

12. Read Philippians 2:5–11, which describes the humble descent that Jesus underwent to live on earth—and even to die on the cross—before he was ultimately exalted to the right hand of God. In what way can the suffering and persecution that David begins experiencing at the hands of Saul in this lesson's passage serve as a picture of this humiliation that Christ experienced before his exaltation?

13. Proverbs 18:24 reminds God's people that a good friend "sticks closer than a brother." How do we see Jonathan providing a beautiful example of Christian friendship in 1 Samuel 20? In what ways does his friendship with David foreshadow the relationship that we have with Jesus Christ, God's Anointed One?

THEOLOGY CONNECTIONS

14. According to answer 28 of the Westminster Larger Catechism, some of the inward effects of sin include "blindness of mind, a reprobate sense, strong delusions, hardness of heart, horror of conscience, and vile affections." How do the words and actions that you see from Saul in this passage's account put these effects of sin on display?

15. Central to Reformed theology is the concept of the *covenant*—an unbreakable promise that God makes to his people that is founded on his gracious will and purpose. How can this concept of the *covenant* be seen throughout 1 Samuel 20's portrayal of the friendship and commitment between Jonathan and David? While theirs is a merely human covenant, how does it point beautifully to the covenant of grace that God has made with his people through his Son Jesus Christ?

APPLYING THE TEXT

16. What can we learn—and what warning can we take—from the fear, anxiety, insecurity, and paranoia that begin to grip King Saul throughout this passage we have been studying? What do these things teach us in particular about what happens to a life and heart that has abandoned the fear of God?

17. How can the way in which David responds to persecution, danger, and even attempts on his life guide you regarding your own response to trials and suffering? In what way should his behavior serve to shape your response to evil that is done to you?

18. David was clearly to endure the *cross* before the *crown*—as was Jesus Christ, the greater David; for both of them, suffering would come before exaltation. What makes this truth important for you, as a follower of Jesus, to remember daily?

PRAYER PROMPT

The passage we have studied for this lesson offers us a strong warning as we observe the deepening darkness, madness, anger, and paranoia that grip Saul's heart and soul after he turns from the Lord. It would be wise for us to pray that God will guard and protect our hearts and will keep us humbly focused on the glory of his Son above all. Pray today, also, for the willingness to embrace your own cross before your crown, in the knowledge that Jesus himself, like David, faced suffering before his exaltation.

A Life of Covenant Faithfulness, pg. 357

Jonathan had liberated himself from the depravity of his father by choosing covenant faithfulness to God over a self-centered grasping after personal ambition. He had come to a living embrace of one of the maxims of Jesus: "Seek first the kingdom of God and his righteousness, and all these things will be added to you" (Matt. 6:33).

LESSON 11

A KING ON THE RUN

1 Samuel 21:1–23:29

THE BIG PICTURE

As we saw in our last lesson, the crippling envy and murderous rage that Saul feels toward David has been intensifying. Despite the deep covenantal friendship that David has with Saul's son Jonathan, Saul's dangerous hatred drives him to the wilderness as he runs and hides out of fear for his life. The passage that we will study today begins with David barging in on Ahimelech the priest and demanding consecrated bread for his men along with the sword of Goliath (21:1–9). He then barely escapes from Gath with his life—after pretending to be insane (21:10–15).

Chapter 22 opens with the moving scene of outcasts and outlaws from all over the land of Israel gathering to David for safety and care as he is at the cave of Adullam (22:1–5). As a stark contrast to this picture, the rest of the chapter reveals how ruthless and evil King Saul's heart has become. Following a report from Doeg the Edomite, who witnessed the aid that Ahimelech offered to David, Saul oversees the brutal murder of eighty-five priests of God (22:6–19). Only Abiathar escapes, and he goes on to find safety with David (22:20–23).

David, even while on the run, delivers the city of Keilah from the attacking Philistines—only to be attacked by Saul and his army just after the battle ends (23:1–14). He continues fleeing from Saul into the wilderness, where Jonathan visits him and offers him encouragement (23:15–18). Saul is called away to a battle against the Philistines just as he is closing in

DAVID,

on David's location (23:19–29). God's anointed king is on the run—but God's hand is preserving him and preparing him for the throne.

Read 1 Samuel 21:1–23:29.

GETTING STARTED

1. What has God taught you through times of fear, trouble, or even danger that you have experienced? What temptations did you face, regarding your actions, your thoughts, or your words, as you went through those times?

2. Why is it so important for Christians to understand the suffering, pain, and temptation that Jesus Christ faced while on the earth? How can knowing these truths about Jesus encourage us when we face the same things that he faced?

The Lord Does Not Let Go of His Servants, pg. 362

As we study David's flight through Nob and refuge in Gath, we will not only consider the folly of a believer gripped by fear, but also learn, as Dale Ralph Davis writes, that "even in their most desperate moments [the Lord] does not let go of his servants, least of all David, his king-elect."

OBSERVING THE TEXT

3. What things does David do and say throughout this passage to show the desperation he is experiencing as a man who is running for his life? What things does he do and say that demonstrate the trust he still has in God—even in the midst of his danger and fear?

4. What stark contrast does 1 Samuel 22 paint between the character of David and the character of Saul? What do outlaws and broken people find in the presence of David? What do religious leaders find in the presence of Saul?

5. What do we continue to learn throughout this passage about the sin, the obsession, and the anger that characterize Saul? What do we learn about the character and faithfulness of God—as well as about the care he shows to David and the plan he has for him?

UNDERSTANDING THE TEXT

6. What aspects of David's conduct in Nob are unholy, dangerous, and potentially harmful to others (21:1–9)? What might this passage be teaching us about his faults and weaknesses?

7. What is humiliating about the method through which David escapes from Gath (21:10–15)? How does God use his embarrassing behavior to deliver him from the Philistines?

8. What kind of people gather around David as 1 Samuel 22 opens—and what kind of welcome does he give them? In what way does this serve as a beautiful picture of how Jesus Christ welcomes sinners and cares for them?

Rallying the Outcast, pg. 375

There are many ways in which David typifies the coming Savior, Jesus Christ. This passage where David rallies the outcast and the unwanted of Israel is an example that is often overlooked, yet it is among the most profound. Like David at Adullam, Jesus gathered a band of followers that the world could describe only as ragtag, and that the Pharisees derided as "tax collectors and sinners" (Matt. 9:11).

9. To what new depths of depravity does Saul descend in 1 Samuel 22:6–19? In what way does this further our understanding of the evil of his heart and his sin against God and his people? What does David do, in contrast to Saul (22:20–23)?

10. Describe David's response to the word he receives from God in 23:1–14. How and when does he inquire of the Lord—and how does he respond to the answer he receives? What makes this behavior very different from what we have been seeing from King Saul?

11. As Saul continues to chase David, what does Jonathan do to encourage David again in the Lord (23:15–18)? What way of escape does God dramatically provide from Saul just as he and his men are about to overtake David (23:19–29)?

BIBLE CONNECTIONS

12. Read Matthew 12:1–8, in which Jesus refers to the visit David made to Ahimelech the priest when he went to Nob. How does Jesus use this account from David's life to point to the true meaning of the Sabbath? What argument is he making about what David did—and about what he himself is doing on the Sabbath day?

13. While David's escape from Gath after acting like a madman receives only six short verses in 1 Samuel, it became a source of the praise he offered God in his life and heart. Read Psalm 34—one of the psalms that he penned after reflecting on God's deliverance. Where in the psalm does he attribute his rescue to God? What effect did this event seem to have on him?

THEOLOGY CONNECTIONS

14. In his great hymn "A Mighty Fortress," Martin Luther writes this about Satan: "Still our ancient foe doth seek to work us woe. His craft and pow'r are great; and, armed with cruel hate, on earth is not his equal." In what way does Saul prove to be similar to this description of Satan as he pursues God's anointed one in the passage we are studying?

15. Central to a Reformed understanding of salvation is the doctrine of *adoption*, which the Westminster Confession of Faith describes in this way: "All those that are justified God vouchsafeth, in and for his only Son Jesus Christ, to make partakers of the grace of adoption; by which they are taken into the number, and enjoy the liberties and privileges of the children of God" (12.1). How could 1 Samuel 22:2 be seen as providing a partial picture of the way God adopts sinners in need?

APPLYING THE TEXT

16. In what ways do times of high stress or desperation tempt you to disobey God's Word or abandon your trust in his purposes? What would help you to better remember to pray, consult God's Word, and calmly trust in him during these times?

17. What is encouraging to you about the Christlike picture that David presents in 1 Samuel 22:1–5 as he welcomes the outlaws and outcasts to himself? How can that picture serve to remind you of, and comfort you with, the beauty of your own salvation?

18. First Samuel 23 makes it clear that David is living his life in submission to what God says and that he consults the Lord before every major decision and endeavor. In what way should this serve as an example to you? What would it look like for you to consult God's Word during the key moments of your life?

PRAYER PROMPT

David is not a perfect man, which we can see clearly from the desperate measures he takes as well as the deception and sometimes rash behavior he engages in. Yet he is a man who has been anointed by God and is learning to seek what God has to say. Pray, today, to be able to consult God's good and true Word more often—and particularly so in times of stress, difficulty, or desperation. Remember that David points us to the perfect King, Jesus Christ. End your study today by praising your Savior for the refuge he provides to needy and helpless sinners like us, who would be hopeless outcasts were it not for his saving mercy and grace.

A Means of Rescue, pg. 391
Like David, when we make a habit of carefully consulting the Lord, not only are we enabled to reign through God's Word, but we are also rescued from all manner of dangers. . . . Christians who diligently consult God's Word will be delivered from great sin.

LESSON 12

A GRACIOUS KING

1 Samuel 24:1–26:25

THE BIG PICTURE

In the previous lesson, we saw that the anointed king is on the run—he is hiding, fighting, and surviving while being pursued by an obsessed king who is filled with envy and murderous hatred. Yet even as Saul ferociously chases him down, God is preserving David and preparing him for the throne. And even during these dangerous days and wilderness years, David comes to embrace the way and words of God more and more.

In the three chapters we will study for this lesson, David is given two separate opportunities to kill Saul—and during both of them he restrains himself from doing so and instead trusts God to accomplish his will in his time. First he spares Saul's life in a cave as the king unwittingly relieves himself near the very place where David is hiding (24:1–21)! Saul retreats with words of apology and swears to cease his murderous pursuit of David (24:22). Before long, though, he is on David's heels again and is chasing him with the help of his soldiers. In an account that echoes the one in the cave that we have just seen two chapters earlier, David creeps unnoticed into Saul's camp as he sleeps, where he finds himself again with an opportunity to take the life of his enemy (26:1–20). Again he shows restraint, which leads Saul to once again confess the "sin" of his pursuit of David and to speak words of blessing to him (26:21–25). Thus David, the anointed one, demonstrates the Christlike qualities of humility, restraint, and trust in God as he refuses to return evil for evil.

103

Wedged between these two accounts of David's sparing of Saul's life is the record of his meeting with Abigail—the wife of the foolish Nabal (25:1–44). In this episode, David nearly slaughters all the men of Nabal in a fit of rage, only to be restrained carefully by a wise and godly woman, who eventually becomes his wife. David is often Christlike, but he is no Christ! Abigail guides him, at a key moment, toward wisdom, restraint, and trust in God's plan.

Read 1 Samuel 24:1–26:25.

GETTING STARTED

1. Have you ever been given a perfect opportunity to take revenge—a chance to *get back* at someone who has wronged you? What makes such an opportunity so enticing? What might hold you back from acting on such an opportunity?

2. When have you seen the great value of showing *restraint*—in examples from either your own life or the lives of others? What makes us respect people who humbly refuse to strike back when they are wronged? How does such behavior remind us of our Savior?

OBSERVING THE TEXT

3. What does David say about God in 1 Samuel 24? How does his view of God—of God's ways and his plan—shape the way in which he responds to the clear opportunity he encounters for taking Saul's life?

4. How does David's demeanor and attitude following the interaction he has with Nabal differ from the demeanor and attitude he displays during his interactions with Saul in 1 Samuel 24 and 26? Why do you think this is the case?

5. What response does Saul give (again) when David spares his life in 1 Samuel 26? Does he seem sincere? What seems to be David's conclusion about Saul's sincerity, when you consider the actions he takes and the response he gives to Saul's words of contrition and blessing?

The Lord's Anointed, pg. 413

David knew that Saul did not remain on the throne by accident, but by God's sovereign will. However little respect David now had for Saul, he had a deep reverence for the office Saul held, seeing it as a manifestation of God's reign. Looking on the situation from the Godward direction, David remembered that Saul was still "the Lord's anointed" (1 Sam. 24:6).

UNDERSTANDING THE TEXT

6. What might be causing David's men to assume that his opportunity to kill Saul in the cave has been given to him by God (24:1–7)? What is different about the way David sees things—and why does he choose to restrain himself from harming Saul?

7. How does David explain to Saul this choice to restrain himself from harming him (24:8–15)? What does he say about the trust he has in God's ultimate justice and ability to act on his behalf? How does Saul respond to David's words in 24:16–22—and does this response surprise you?

8. What makes the response Nabal gives to David's request so incredibly foolish (25:1–13)? How does David's response serve to make his fury obvious? What character faults might this response to Nabal's incendiary words be exposing within David?

A Gracious Ministry, pg. 433

Abigail's wise approach to David not only averted disaster. Her actions also remind us of the gospel of salvation that comes to us upon the path of unbelief, sin, and destruction. Abigail is not formally a type of Christ in the same manner David was. Yet her gracious ministry to David presents strong analogies to the grace by which Jesus meets us and brings us to salvation.

9. Describe what you observe in 25:14–44 about the wisdom, character, and grace of Abigail. What makes her an exemplary character in this book of the Bible—one who even resembles Jesus Christ in many ways? In what way does she deliver David from rash sin and violence? How does God's ultimate judgment fall on Nabal—and how does this serve to further validate the path that Abigail took rather than the one that David intended to take?

10. What does Saul's subsequent pursuit of David reveal about the lack of change that has taken place in his heart (26:1–2)? What additional opportunity does David receive for killing Saul in 26:3–12—only to stop short of taking his life yet again?

11. Read 1 Samuel 26:13–25 again. What is David seeking to prove about his character through both the actions he takes and the words he speaks to King Saul (vv. 17–20)? In what way does Saul respond, and what does he acknowledge about his own sin and about the worthiness of David when he does so (vv. 21–25)? How do Saul's words show us that David is a clear type of Jesus Christ?

BIBLE CONNECTIONS

12. Read the words Jesus speaks in Matthew 26:52–54 after Peter has struck out with his sword against the high priest's servant in Jesus's defense (as corroborated by John 18:10). How does Jesus display godly restraint? What purpose does he say is behind this restraint?

13. In Philippians 2:6–7 (NIV), the apostle Paul tells us that Jesus Christ "did not count equality with God a thing to be grasped" but instead chose to make himself "nothing" by taking the nature of a "servant" during his descent to earth and death on the cross. How does our passage for this lesson portray David resisting the urge to "grasp" *his* kingdom as well—and how do the years of humble wandering that he spends in the wilderness point us forward to Jesus in their own way?

THEOLOGY CONNECTIONS

14. John Calvin suggests that, just as "it is not lawful to usurp the office of God, it is not lawful to revenge; for we thus anticipate the judgment of God, who will have this office reserved for himself."[1] In what way do the actions that David takes in 1 Samuel 24 and 26 bear out Calvin's assertion? How do the words he speaks affirm his confidence in the judgment of God as well?

---

1. John Calvin, *St. Paul's Epistle to the Romans*, trans. John King, The John Calvin Bible Commentaries (repr., North Charleston, SC: Createspace, 2015), 246.

15. Answer 35 of the Westminster Shorter Catechism tells us, "Sanctification is the work of God's free grace, whereby we are renewed in the whole man after the image of God, and are enabled more and more to die unto sin, and live unto righteousness." In what way does David's initial reaction to Nabal's rude words in 1 Samuel 25:13 demonstrate his need for ongoing sanctification in his life?

APPLYING THE TEXT

16. In 1 Samuel 24, we see David not only resisting his *own* temptation to kill Saul and seize the kingdom but also resisting pressure from his *friends* to kill Saul. How could this serve as a challenge to you to stand strong when friends or coworkers pressure you in a sinful direction?

17. What actions and attitudes that we have seen from Abigail in this lesson might you seek to emulate? How can she serve as an example for you of wisdom, humility, and godly counsel?

No Crowns without Crosses, pg. 421

Are you tempted to seek the crown of salvation without the cross of a life governed by obedience to God's Word? Are you tempted to justify sinful or worldly means because the outward results will come more easily? May God grant us the power, along with David, looking at the crucified and resurrected Jesus, never to lay our hands on the blessings that God has promised in a manner contrary to the will of God in his Word.

18. While his encounter with Nabal reminds us that David is far from perfect, in what way does he demonstrate the merciful and gracious heart of Jesus in 1 Samuel 24 and 26? What makes this specifically encouraging to you in the context of your walk with the Lord?

PRAYER PROMPT

As you close today's study of these three chapters of 1 Samuel, praise God that you know the Savior to whom David points. Jesus is the King who shows mercy toward his enemies—even dying to save those who hate him until God's grace opens their hearts in faith. Pray that you, too, will show mercy to those who seek to wrong you or do you harm. Ask God for the strength to trust that he will accomplish his good purposes in your life according to his perfect timing.

LESSON 13

THE FALL AND RISE OF KINGS

1 Samuel 27:1–31:13

THE BIG PICTURE

David, God's anointed king over his people Israel, has been on the run from the envious and murderous King Saul. Twice David has mercifully spared Saul's life—refusing to kill him when given the opportunity and choosing instead to trust that God will judge Saul in his time. David has also found for himself a godly wife: Abigail, who provided wise and godly counsel to him when he was bent on violent revenge.

This final lesson will cover a large section of text—five chapters in all. You will study the final days of David's wilderness years as well as the final downfall and death of King Saul, who descends into tragic despair, sin, and darkness. In 1 Samuel 27, David finds a surprising place of refuge: the land of the Philistines (27:1–12). Yet in contrast with David, to whom God grants safety even in the land of his enemies, Saul finds only silence from God. He does the unthinkable; he chooses to inquire of a medium (or witch), through whom he receives a vision and final word of judgment from the dead prophet Samuel (28:1–25). Having been told about his impending death, Saul eats a sad final meal—a means of gathering the strength to go into battle and die. Then, after David is ultimately rejected by the Philistines with whom he had temporarily found refuge but who now distrust him (29:1–11), we read of his dramatic rescue of the wives and families of his men, who have been captured by the Amalekites (30:1–31). He shows grace and generosity as a leader by sharing the spoils with all of his men—even the ones who were too exhausted to complete the conquest and fight the Amalekite soldiers. Finally, the book of 1 Samuel concludes with a very sad day for Israel, as King Saul and his son Jonathan are both killed in battle against the Philistines (31:1–13). Saul's death is followed by humiliation, as his dismembered body is displayed in a Philistine temple, where it is ultimately rescued and buried by the loyal citizens of Jabesh-gilead.

Read 1 Samuel 27:1–31:13.

GETTING STARTED

1. During times of waiting, frustration, or suffering, what tempts you to cling to lesser hopes instead of to God himself? What idols do you find most appealing during difficult times, and in what way do you tend to look to those things for comfort, security, and safety?

2. Why is the reality of God's judgment—and the reality of eternal punishment—so difficult for present-day people to accept? What might people be failing to understand about the reality of sin when they can't accept these things? In what way do they tend to underestimate the holiness of God?

OBSERVING THE TEXT

3. Do you notice a pattern in the way these chapters are organized? Why might the narrator of 1 Samuel keep switching back and forth between the accounts of David and of Saul as the king of Israel's reign approaches its end?

4. In what ways does David demonstrate a failure of faith and a lack of trust in God throughout these chapters? What makes it evident that God is protecting and blessing his anointed future king—even when he faces danger and makes foolish decisions?

5. What about King Saul is meant to warn us, sadden us, and even frighten us? (Note especially chapters 28 and 31.) Why might God have chosen to include these accounts of King Saul for his people to read for generations to come?

A Tragic End to an Impenitent Life, pg. 510

As we come to the end of the Bible's account of Israel's King Saul, and to the end of Saul's life, it is not hard to see that the dominant theme of his life was his hard-hearted impenitence. . . . Sadly, Saul's life was a bitter record of God's way forsaken and God's pardon forfeited by his refusal to repent. . . . There could be only one end for such a life as Saul's, an end as tragic as it is unnecessary for those who have witnessed the grace and power of God.

UNDERSTANDING THE TEXT

6. What seems to motivate David's decision to seek safety in the land of the Philistines (27:1)? How could his actions throughout 27:1–12 be interpreted as betraying a lack of trust in God as well as a failure to rest in the promises that God made to him?

7. How does the beginning of 1 Samuel 28 make it evident that God has fully abandoned Saul (28:1–7)? What makes verse 6 such a sad, striking, and somber verse—and how does it demonstrate God's judgment against Saul?

8. What is so ironic about the visit Saul makes to the medium (28:3, 9)? What message does Samuel give to him on God's behalf (28:15–19)? In what way does the final meal that Saul eats contrast with the last supper of Jesus Christ? What dark day lies ahead for Saul—and what dark day came after Jesus's final meal with his disciples?

9. How does 1 Samuel 29 make it evident that God's grace is on David's life—especially through the way he is removed at the last second from the army of the Philistines as they prepare to fight against Israel? What does the fact that David was preparing for battle *alongside* the Philistines against the Israelite army tell us about his mindset, attitude, and heart?

Or do you believe he was perhaps planning to turn against the Philistines unexpectedly during the battle (see verse 8 and its potentially hidden meaning)?

10. What is especially desperate about David's situation as the following chapter begins (30:1–6)? In what way does God use his military strength to bring deliverance to him and his men (30:7–20)? How does David show Christlike mercy and generosity at the conclusion of the battle—even against the urging of his men (30:21–31)?

11. What is particularly dishonorable and sad about the death that Saul dies in battle (31:1–7)? What might be the motivation behind the actions the men of Jabesh-gilead take as they "rescue" Saul's body (31:8–13)? What do we learn about the judgment of God, and about the wages of sin and rebellion, from Saul's demise?

Entering the Darkness, pg. 482

How great—how infinitely great—was the difference between Saul in the darkness of his own sin and Jesus in the darkness of sins he did not commit. Saul, with his hardened heart and in his rebellion against God, had entered a darkness that would last forever in hell. But the Savior entered the darkness of condemnation in order that he might take its curse away forever from the people who belong to him in faith.

BIBLE CONNECTIONS

12. Read Amos 8:11–12. What particular judgment does the prophet declare that God will bring on his people? In what way is it similar to the judgment that King Saul receives in 1 Samuel 28:6?

13. In Matthew 20:1–16, Jesus tells a parable about workers in a field who all receive the same wages even though they work for different lengths of time. Glance through that parable now. What lesson is Jesus teaching in it about God's grace and his kingdom? What similarities do you see between the principle he is teaching here and what David mandates in 1 Samuel 30:23–25?

THEOLOGY CONNECTIONS

14. Reformed theologians speak and write often about the *providence* of God, by which he ordains everything that comes to pass, including the decisions of world rulers and empires, for his glory and his people's good. What evidence of God's providence do you see throughout the account that 1 Samuel 27 and 29 contain of David's stay in the land of the Philistines?

15. Answer 52 of the Heidelberg Catechism describes the *comfort* we can take from the doctrine of the final judgment with these words: "With uplifted head I look for the very same Person who before has offered Himself for my sake to the tribunal of God, and has removed all curse

from me, to come as Judge from heaven; who shall cast all His and my enemies into everlasting condemnation, but shall take me with all His chosen ones to Himself into heavenly joy and glory." In what way was God's judgment upon King Saul ultimately good news for Israel?

APPLYING THE TEXT

16. David is God's anointed king, but he certainly fails to show a perfect trust in God in this passage—most notably when he seeks shelter and safety in the land of the idolatrous Philistines. How can this serve as a warning to us about our own idolatrous tendency to shelter ourselves in places other than Christ alone?

17. What Christlike qualities do we see in David, even when he is in the midst of the failures he experiences in these chapters? How should the way he behaves toward his exhausted men in 30:23–25 encourage us regarding the heart that God's greater King, Jesus, has for us?

A Concluding Act of Courage, pg. 519

The fact that 1 Samuel ends with a courageous act of gratitude toward Saul says more about God than it does about Saul. It reminds us that even the worst of lives has borne the image of God and has shared at least sparks of God's goodness and love. This concluding note also shows how eager God is to bless and reward the least acts of faith and obedience. Even the death of Saul provides us with an incentive to repent of our sins, turn to the Lord in true faith, and serve the Lord.

18. While Saul's death serves as a stern warning for those who fail to repent and listen to what God says, it also reminds us of the many opportunities for repentance that Saul was given. How should 1 Samuel 31 serve to drive you toward humble repentance and faith in Jesus?

PRAYER PROMPT

As this lesson brings you to the tragic end of the life of King Saul, take some time to engage in personal repentance and heart-searching prayer before God. Ask him to gently point out sinful attitudes, thoughts, and pursuits in your life so that you may turn to him in humility and repentance. Then praise God for his faithfulness in the areas of both his judgment of his enemies and his preservation of his people. Thank him for the steadfast plan he made to set up his true, good King over his people—even the great Son of David, your Savior.

Jon Nielson is senior pastor of Spring Valley Presbyterian Church in Roselle, Illinois, and the author of *Bible Study: A Student's Guide*, among other books. He has served in pastoral positions at Holy Trinity Church, Chicago, and College Church, Wheaton, Illinois, and as director of training for the Charles Simeon Trust.

Richard D. Phillips (MDiv, Westminster Theological Seminary; DD, Greenville Presbyterian Theological Seminary) is the senior minister of Second Presbyterian Church of Greenville, South Carolina. He is a council member of the Alliance of Confessing Evangelicals and of The Gospel Coalition and chairman of the Philadelphia Conference on Reformed Theology.

P&R PUBLISHING'S COMPANION COMMENTARY

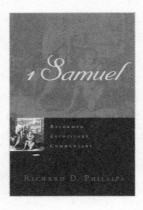

"Rick Phillips has provided the church with another indispensable tool in this expository commentary on 1 Samuel. He carefully addresses and pastorally handles the memorable narratives of Samuel, Saul, and David and gives special attention to character development, historical background, sound doctrine, and practical application." —**Steven J. Lawson**

The Reformed Expository Commentary (REC) series is accessible to both pastors and lay readers. Each volume in the series provides exposition that gives careful attention to the biblical text, is doctrinally Reformed, focuses on Christ through the lens of redemptive history, and applies the Bible to our contemporary setting.

Praise for the Reformed Expository Commentary Series

"Well-researched and well-reasoned, practical and pastoral, shrewd, solid, and searching." —**J. I. Packer**

"A rare combination of biblical insight, theological substance, and pastoral application." —**Al Mohler**

"Here, rigorous expository methodology, nuanced biblical theology, and pastoral passion combine." —**R. Kent Hughes**